Hints for Lay Preachers

By

F. B. MEYER

Author of "The Shepherd Psalm," "Lovers Alway,"
"Our Daily Homily," etc.

NEW YORK   CHICAGO   TORONTO

Fleming H. Revell Company

LONDON AND EDINBURGH

SECOND EDITION.

PREFACE

On each Lord's day large numbers of devoted men, who have not received special training for their noble work, go forth to preach the unsearchable riches of Christ.

It is impossible to overestimate the worth of their self-sacrificing labours. Thousands of pulpits in town and country would stand empty and silent but for them. And the standard of excellence set before them and realised is very high.

I have put together these chapters in as brief a form as possible, because I am addressing busy men; but they contain the results of a good deal of experience and observation, and they come with much cordial esteem to those whom I may fitly claim as brethren and fellow-workers in the gospel of our Lord.

F. B. MEYER.

AUGUSTINE'S CREED

A whole Christ for my Salvation.
A whole Bible for my Staff.
A whole Church for my Fellowship.
A whole World for my Parish.

CONTENTS

" It's a Coal from God's Altar must kindle our Fire: And without Fire, true Fire, no acceptable sacrifice."

WILLIAM PENN.

JOTTINGS AND HINTS

FOR LAY PREACHERS

———+———

I

BE SURE OF YOUR MESSAGE

THERE is all the difference possible between delivering a sermon and uttering a message.

In the first instance, you feel much as a lecturer or professor who receives a definite salary for definite work. It may be very interesting and congenial work, engaging his whole soul, and filling him with pride and thankfulness—still, it is work, and it is expected of him. At a certain hour he is due at a certain spot, where his audience awaits him, and he must do his best to instruct and interest the people until the hands of the clock have revolved to a given point.

There is a tendency in some preachers to view their work in this way. They have an appointment; their names are down on a preaching list; or the stated demands of their pulpit appeal to them. It is necessary to speak for half an hour, more or less, on some sacred theme—it doesn't much matter what. They begin to think over subjects; they casually open volumes of sermons to obtain the suggestions of other men's minds; they look over lists of likely texts which they have jotted down in their note-books. Ultimately they come to the conclusion that they can make something of a given subject; or a text is suggested which is capable of bright and original treatment; or the next paragraph in their scheme of scriptural exposition claims thoughtful treatment. Thereupon they laboriously accumulate all the light and information which can be obtained from such authors as are within their reach, collate their thoughts into some kind of order, and with much pains write out, or in some other way prepare, their discourse. This may be good, elaborate, and interesting, but when it is preached it fails to grip the hearers; it resembles a glass of mineral water, once bubbling and sparkling, but, through standing long, the special effervescence which constituted its attractiveness has entirely passed away.

We would not for a moment affirm that sermons made in this way do not realise a purpose, and are not used for the conversion and edification of the souls of men; but only that they do not realise the

highest ideal of what a sermon may be, when it is
delivered as a message from the Most High.

It was stated in a newspaper paragraph which I
came across the other day, that a certain foreign
hypnotist had been of considerable service to various
clergymen who had resorted to him because he
impressed them with the idea that they were God's
mouthpiece, and that the Divine Spirit was speaking through them; but surely it is not needful to
call in the assistance of hypnotism to imbue us
with such a thought as that. It was simply the
ordinary position that was assumed by each of the
holy men who spoke for God in the old time, and
which was the perpetual standpoint of the apostles.

Take, for instance, Acts xv. 12: "Barnabas and
Paul rehearsed what signs and wonders God had
wrought *through* them"; also Rom. xv. 18: "I
will not dare to speak of any things save those
which Christ wrought *through* me for the obedience
of the Gentiles." Everything depends on our
entering deeply into the meaning of that preposition,
and whether we work for God or realise that God
is working in and through us.

I remember well one of the most widely used
evangelists in the United States standing up before
a great gathering of brother ministers and testify-
ing that his whole life had been altered by seeing
a sentence in an address of mine, delivered at

Northfield, in which I insisted that our usefulness in God's service was largely affected by the question, whether we worked for God, or allowed God by His Spirit to speak and work through us. He knelt down beside his study table and vowed that from that hour he would yield himself to be the medium and instrument by which the divine words should be spoken and His will effected; and the result was a vast increase in his power and usefulness. When that position has been taken up, the one desire of the servant of God is to realise that he is intrusted with a message, that his address to his congregation is not that of an advocate, but of a witness, and that he is the medium of passing on the special burden of the Lord. We would not say that they who prepare their sermons after the former manner are not also the messengers of the Lord of Hosts; but he who waits in prayer and faith before God, that he may be charged with a message, is pre-eminently such.

We obtain such a message in prayer when we wait upon God, or when dealing with some specific cases of spiritual difficulty. Sometimes I have found that the newspapers, either religious or secular, and the monthly periodicals, which have revealed some tendency of current thought or the growing prevalence of some special form of wickedness, have laid on my soul the sense of responsibility to speak the divine message so far as I have been able to catch and reflect it.

As to the form in which the message is stated, that needs careful and thoughtful elaboration. We have no right to deliver the divine thought in a slipshod or slovenly manner. The apple of gold must be set in the frame of silver. The King's words must be engrossed on parchment or vellum. There must be a full use of every method which would enhance to others the sense of the glory and claims of Him for whom we speak.

Preach all your sermons over to yourself. Remember that your own heart must ever be your first congregation. Take for yourself, that you may know if it be digestible, some of the food which you are preparing for others.

II

ONE AIM AND PURPOSE

THE longer I live, and study the effect of sermons and speeches, the more sure I am that it is a profound mistake to introduce too many divergent themes, any one of which is useful and interesting, but none stands out with such marked prominence and distinctness as to arrest the attention of the congregation.

What a contrast there is between the styles of some preachers and that of the barrister. They talk about their subject, and say many pretty and edifying things, which sound well, and would read well, which are pleasantly conceived and elegantly expressed. They walk about Zion, and go round about her, telling her towers, and considering her palaces, but they do not dream of making a breach in her walls, and carrying them by an assault. The other fixes on some salient point in his brief which is capable of being driven home, as a wedge to split a tree. However far he may seem from it, he always returns to it at last; and the jury leave the box with one thought or fact that demands consideration, and becomes the standpoint from which they view the whole case.

Surely the latter is the truer method, and the more effective. He is a successful preacher of the highest order who manages to present one great conception before his people each time he addresses them, so that, as they break from the spell of his influence, they may be possessed by one thought, inspired by one motive, and compelled towards one act.

Two of the greatest preachers of modern times, Mr. Spurgeon and Phillips Brooks, though so different in almost every other respect, were alike in this, that each of their sermons would gather round one central thought, which burnt itself into brain and heart. Mr. Spurgeon would show how that one thought appeared under the light of each of the doctrines of grace, how it had to do with every possible experience, how it solved every kind of difficulty. As you listened to him, you began to realise the importance of some fragment of truth which you had previously hardly considered. For the moment, it filled the entire horizon of your soul. You ruminated about it, spoke of it, began to find it for yourself everywhere, and felt permanently richer. So with the great Boston preacher: his sermons are delightful models of what each of us should aim at (I will not stand sponsor for all his theology) in the presentation of truth. In the first one or two paragraphs he states the truth which he has discovered in his text, and begins to illustrate and enforce it by references to that world of men of which he was so accurate an observer.

In the beginning of our ministry, our sermons are crowded with too many differing thoughts, suggestions, and references to foreign objects; we fear that we shall not last out; we hurry from one subject to another, as the bee flits from flower to flower. At the close of our address our hearers have but a vague and hazy conception of what we have been speaking about; they may feel that it has all been very good, but they have no definite conception left with them, and they certainly do not feel compelled, as the Athenians were after hearing Demosthenes, "to go and fight Philip."

Let it be clearly borne in mind that a redundancy of thought may be a great cause of weakness in a sermon. Everything that detracts from the main end in view should be carefully eschewed and cut out; and the current of thought should be kept within as narrow a channel as possible, that it may flow swiftly, and move the machinery along its banks.

This type of preaching makes heavier demands on careful preparation than that which is more discursive. Every new paragraph has to be weighed, and its place carefully considered, with the view of ascertaining whether it will add cogency to the argument and force to the appeal. But at the same time it will suggest lines of argument and side-lights of illustration which will be fresh, vivid, and illuminating. We are all tempted to put an illustration or piece of scenery into our sermons because it is striking and picturesque; and there is often no reason to bar such things from entrance. But no true preacher who had adopted the ideal for which we are arguing would admit such pleas for a moment. With merciless rigour he would cut out every piece of needless rhetoric, as the great artist struck the exquisitely painted chalice out of his picture of the Lord's Supper, because it attracted attention which he meant to focus on the face of Christ. But when you have a point before you which you want to make clear and operative to your hearers, as you revolve it you will be glad to catch at the assistance of incidents and illustrations which you would not employ for their beauty or pathos, but which admirably serve the purpose you have in view. You refrain from using anything that will not really illuminate,

2

and enforce, and add to the power of your appeal.

It might be supposed that the methodical expositor of the Bible would be unable to model his discourses on this pattern. But it is not so. It is always possible, in a paragraph of Scripture, to discover the one pivot-sentence on which the whole context turns, and around which every clause may be grouped. Let this be announced as the text, and the attention of every thoughtful person will be enlisted to see how central and pertinent the selected clause is to the remainder of the paragraph.

In every sermon we should present our theme to the intellect with a thoughtful exposition of its truth; to the imagination, that it may be seen under the prismatic lens; to the conscience, that it may receive the sanction and acquiescence of what is best in man; to the heart, that the fountain of emotion may be deeply stirred; to the will, that it may be forced to take sides, and choose. Take your wares, oh, heavenly merchant-man, to each door in Mansoul. Perchance, if one is barred against you, another may be opened. Only take no refusal, and persist in the reiteration from every key, and instrument, and dialect, of the one message which the Spirit has laid upon your soul.

III

THE PREACHER'S OBJECTIVE

ONE of the greatest texts which illuminate the apostle's practice and suggests our own is that in which he said that he was not anxious to commend himself, or furnish letters of commendation, because he sought by the manifestation of the truth to commend himself to every man's conscience in the sight of God. The poet appeals to the imagination, the essayist to the sense of culture, the logician to the intellect, and if, as preachers, we vie with any of these, we expose ourselves to certain disappointment. The true preacher passes by them all, and though he is not indifferent to the claims of fancy, art, and thought, he strikes at the spiritual life of men, and appeals to their conscience in the sight of God. The conscience is our true objective. It is little for us, therefore, that men should say they are pleased with our discourses, or have enjoyed our sermons. We can never rest satisfied with such phrases as these. If they sum up the whole effect of our work, we may hang our heads in shame and feel that we have failed. It is only when we have so wrought with God that the conscience has been pricked and stirred, or led to yield its willing or unwilling testimony to the truth of our statements, that we can feel that the true object of our mission has been attained.

The following illustration has always appeared to me to set forth the relation which we should hold with conscience.

On his way back from the Crusades, Richard I. was entrapped by his enemies, and imprisoned in a lonely castle in Austria. His subjects were wholly in ignorance as to his whereabouts, and it seemed as though it would be impossible to discover their lost monarch. He had, however, a favourite minstrel, Blondin, who had composed many songs with Richard, and he started forth to play the familiar tunes which they loved in common, beneath the prison walls of the chief castles in Europe. After a weary search he was at last rewarded by hearing a responsive strain come back from a dungeon cell, in which he recognised his master's voice and touch. This led finally to Richard's recovery of liberty and kingdom.

Is not this an illustration of what happens while the Christian minister and preacher, with the instrument of the Word of God in his hand, tells the story of the love of God, reasons of righteousness, temperance, and judgment to come? From within the heart of man, the voice of conscience answers back, note for note, bar for bar. The Word of God finds us at deeper depths than any other book, and thus proves itself to have come from Him who constituted our moral nature. The deep of our moral nature calls to the deep of the Word of God. Oh, minstrels of the gospel story, sing it before the dark dungeons in which the consciences of men are imprisoned until there be a response that shall be the best vindication that you are servants of the Most High!

Once when I was preaching in the Free Church Assembly Hall in Edinburgh, at the close of the afternoon address, I heard two ladies as they descended the staircase saying to one another, "Was it not beautiful?" However gratifying the testimony was in one way, in another it filled me with a sense of failure, because I knew that so searching an address as I had delivered should have led to self-examination and prayer rather than to such a remark as that. So in the evening I introduced my sermon by saying that I was sorry to have failed so absolutely in the afternoon; and when a look of surprise passed over the faces of my audience I explained the ground of my remark, adding, "When a patient has left the operating-room and his flesh is freshly quivering from the surgeon's knife, you hardly expect him to say 'How beautiful it was!' but rather, 'How searching, how painful; yet how glad I am to have endured the knife, if it saved me from a lingering death!' And when Jacob limped into the camp and entered Rachel's tent, on the morning after his wrestling with the angel, we cannot imagine him saying, 'Oh, wife, I have had such a lovely and beautiful night!' but rather, 'Wife, I have passed through an experience which I shall never forget. I shall limp till my dying day, and shall never be quite the same again, but I realise that henceforth there are possibilities within my reach which could not have been, had I not known those hours of awful agony.'"

Am I not speaking that which every true man knows to be right when I say that in our best moods it matters little to us that the people go out from our services passing high encomiums on our eloquence, learning, or faculty for interesting them? The one supreme authentication which we desire is that men should be pricked to the heart and cry out in the throes of conscience, "What must I do to be saved?"

The word "conscience" is derived from the Latin, and means literally "to know with," that is, it deals with what a man knows with himself. Other definitions have been given. Our conscience

has been described as our "self-knowledge, of acts,
or states, or character, as to right or wrong," or
"the faculty which decides upon the lawfulness
or unlawfulness of our actions," or "the judgment
which we pronounce upon our actions or states,
whether the judgment be true or false." The
Bible speaks of it under the emblem of a lamp,
whose light searches the hidden and dark places of
the soul. But perhaps it is better to think of conscience not as one separate substantial faculty of
our nature, but as rather "the sum total of all our
faculties." It is a soul conscious of itself, and
passing judgment upon its own states and actions.
It is the judgment-seat of Christ set up in our
nature. It is the Great White Throne in miniature.
It is a premonition and presage of the Last Assize.
It is the voice of Nathan saying to David, "Thou
art the man," or the reproving figure of Elijah at
the gate of Naboth's vineyard. For long years it
may be stupefied, gagged, neglected, resisted, but
whenever it hears the word of truth proclaimed in
the power of the Spirit of God it stirs again and
awakens. It always recognises the sound of truth
for which it was made. Concerning the expediency
or inexpediency of an action, conscience has nothing
to say. Whether a certain course be wise or the
reverse is a matter on which conscience offers no
opinion; but when it is a question of right or

wrong, conscience arises, and, without hesitation, like another John the Baptist in the palace of Herod, cries, "It is not lawful; it is not right." What an ally this is to the summons of the King of kings at the gateway of the soul—our willing coadjutor, our Heaven-sent confederate!

The old school men, of whom Thomas Aquinas was one, were wont to divide the judging function of the conscience into eight parts :—

1. Conscience *testifies*. It renders a witness concerning this or that state, this or that action, and announces whether it is good or bad.

2. It *obliges*, that is, it acquaints the will with its duty, and declares that the thing which it points out is bound to be undertaken.

3. It *instigates*, inciting the soul in the right direction.

4. It *accuses*, enumerating our offences, and pointing out the details and circumstances of our evil deeds.

5. It *excuses*, declaring that this or the other action is unnecessary.

6. It *blames*, pressing home upon the sinner that it is his fault, and his alone, which has brought about his vile condition.

7. *It causes remorse.*

8. *It pronounces sentence.*

These distinctions have been lately insisted upon

by a noted evangelist, and I think they deserve to be carefully pondered by us; as also the old Eastern tale about the magic ring, which is quoted in the same connection. Placed upon the finger of the sultan by a wandering fakir, this ring possessed the power of being able to prick its wearer whenever he was tempted to do wrong. The hidden lancet from within its sheath, in a mysterious manner, advertised the sultan when he was in danger of committing an injustice. Conscience is that ring, notifying us of the quality of our actions in advance, and always after some offence has been committed. Its universality is of the highest importance. As a Greek orator said, it speaks one language at Athens and Rome, and has a sanction in every heart, and therefore, wherever we go, we are sure of an ally in the breast of Eastern and Western, learned and ignorant, young and old.

In the preparation of your sermons be sure to consider how far they may arouse the conscience; and notice that the apostle distinctly affirms that we shall do this best " by the manifestation of the truth." It is not necessary for us to argue the truth or prove the truth, it is sufficient to attest it, to manifest it, to explain its peculiar bearings; and as certainly as we hold up the truth before men it will work its own effect in its unadorned majesty and strength.

Let us be indifferent to letters of commendation. Let us count it a matter of unconcern whether men are pleased or otherwise. Let our one aim be so to act "in the sight of God" that the conscience of our hearers may accuse or excuse them, and bear testimony that in holiness and godly sincerity, not in fleshly wisdom, but the grace of God, we have behaved ourselves and spoken.

Remember always those words of Chrysostom : "' Feed my sheep.' Not to priests only is this said, but to every one of us also, who are also entrusted with a little flock. But do not despise it because it is a little flock. For 'My Father,' He saith, ' hath pleasure in them.' Each of us hath a sheep; let him lead that to the proper pasture."

IV

THE DEMONSTRATION OF THE SPIRIT

IT is interesting to watch a well-managed lecture at the Royal Institution or elsewhere. Whilst the lecturer is proceeding with his discourse, explaining to his audience the laws of light or sound or the combination of gases, his assistant conducts the practical experiments that appeal to the eye, and demonstrate the truth of what is being advanced.

Similarly, when we have lantern mission services on Sunday evenings at Christ Church, my secretary and I work out a subject between us, and he obtains the loan of illustrative slides, which he casts on the screen, one after another, as I reach the special point of my talk which requires illustration. Whilst I have been addressing the people as well as I could, behind me the same truths have been presented to the eye, so that every word has been substantiated by two witnesses.

In the same way, when the preacher is delivering the message with which God has intrusted him, he has a perfect right to count on the fellowship and co-witness of the Spirit of God, according to the promise of our Lord. Did He not say that the Comforter should bear witness to His truth and glory, and that His disciples should do the same? (John xv. 26, 27). Did not the apostles realise the fulfilment of that mighty assurance, when before the Sanhedrim they cried, "We are witnesses of these things, and so is also the Holy Spirit, whom God hath given to them that obey Him"? (Acts v. 32). Are we not assured that on the first great missionary journey, as Barnabas and Paul spoke boldly in the name of the Lord, that He bore witness to the word of His grace? (Acts xiv. 3). And is it not written that God Himself bore witness to the earliest preachers of the gospel by signs and wonders, and by gifts of the Holy Spirit, according to His own will? (Heb. ii. 4).

Surely these passages, which might be largely matched from all parts of the Bible, go to show that the almighty Spirit waits to corroborate and confirm, to substantiate and enforce every word of His faithful messenger. Just as our Lord was conscious ever that His Father was bearing witness to His words (John v. 36), so every devoted servant of His may reckon on His standing beside, and bearing witness, and giving the seal and demonstration of the Holy Spirit. This is surely what the Apostle Paul meant when he reminded the Thessalonians that the gospel came to them not in word only, but also in power, and in the Holy Spirit, and in much assurance (1 Thess. i. 5).

It may seem like straining the passage, but I almost think that it will bear the interpretation, when we find another statement of the same great fact in Revelation xiv. 13. The beloved disciple first hears a great voice from heaven proclaiming a truth of immense interest and importance; and suddenly he detects another voice asseverating the same blessed truth from amid the heart of the Church—" Yea, saith the Spirit." A friend, knowing how much these words meant to me, illuminated them, and they hang framed on my vestry wall. I trust that I may never say aught from my pulpit to which the Holy Spirit shall be unable to affix His yea, and it would be the most desirable of all attestations if to each message delivered from that or any other pulpit the Holy Spirit might be able to add, whilst the sermon was in process of delivery, His deliberate, emphatic, and spirit-thrilling Amen.

When He, the Spirit of truth, is come, said our Lord, He will convince the world of sin, righteousness, and judgment; and when is He so likely to do this as when His chosen messenger is delivering His truth and using the Word of God, which is His sword? It seems as though our mental and spiritual attitude during the delivery of a sermon must be one of constant expectation; that our Divine Ally, who has also been at His work by our side, will drive home His word with irresistible power, to the dividing asunder of soul and spirit, of the joints and marrow, discerning and criticising the thoughts and intents of each heart. Especially when one is unusually conscious of one's weakness and inability to make the desired impression, one turns to Him, crying, "Put on Thine extraordinary might, oh blessed Spirit, since I am more weak than usual; let Thy might be perfected in my weakness; be more than sufficient to compensate for my failure. My edge is blunt; I lean, therefore, more heavily on Thee; fail not of Thy purpose."

When we are preaching under the deep impression of the Spirit's fellowship, or, as the apostle puts it, of "the communion of the Holy Spirit," we are almost indifferent to the presence or absence of certain people, or to the largeness or smallness of our congregation. Our one aim is to please Him who has chosen us as His associates in the work of glorifying the Lord Jesus, to glorify whom He has come to reside in the heart of the Church.

And when the sermon is ended, we are not anxious to obtain the plaudits of our fellows. If all men applaud us, we are dissatisfied if we miss His assurance that we have wrought with Him.

If all men are silent, yet if He tell us that He is well pleased, we ask no further tribute.

It is impossible to describe the sense of rest and peace which overspreads the soul when a man begins to live like this. He becomes quieter in his manner. Aforetime he supposed that he could best enforce his meaning by shouting aloud, by vigorous gesticulation, and by peculiar mannerisms, which really distracted and worried the audience. One of the most celebrated actors has left his opinion on record, that gesticulation distracts people from catching the sense of the words that are being spoken.[1] This is strikingly true, and when one is conscious that the Spirit is present, accompanying the word with signs and wonders in the hearts and lives of those present, one is apt to become more quiet, self-possessed, and natural. Again those old words come to mind—so deep and true, so restful and quieting—"Not by might, nor by power, but by My Spirit, saith the Lord of Hosts."

---

[1] Macready records in his diary that he lost hold of his audience in a certain scene, and he attributed this to excess of gesture. On this account he determined to go through the same scene the next night with his hands behind him. The result was a great success.

V

"WORKERS TOGETHER" WITH GOD

In my early ministry I was greatly hindered by a leading man in the church—rather vain and self-opinionated—who used to stand at the bottom of the pulpit stairs at the close of the Sunday morning's sermon, and welcome me as I came down with the words, "That was a splendid effort this morning." It was very flattering, and his words continually proved an incentive in the composition of my sermons, that by the glowing rhetoric, the introduction of poetry, and brilliant quotations, I might secure for myself the coveted eulogy. If the well-known sentence were missing for two or three Sundays, I was aroused to keen anxiety, and wrought with my utmost industry and care to obtain the pleasure of its sweet fragrance. Indeed, I am afraid that I sometimes went to his house, and took supper with him on Sunday night, with the one hope that I should be able to extract from him words of similar commendation.

As I look back on it now I feel ashamed that I

could ever have prostituted my opportunities—the ministry of Christ's gospel—to such an unholy purpose. I used the pulpit as an opportunity for ministering to my own vanity and self-congratulation. May God forgive me! But let every preacher who reads these words be warned. Let each, as in a mirror, see the temptation to which he is exposed. We are none of us beyond the temptation of preaching to one or two special people in the audience, for whose delectation we prepare our discourses, whose presence or absence makes all the difference to us in delivering them, and whose word of commendation is greatly desired at the close.

Yet it is obvious that it is good for every preacher to have an incentive, that in preparing beforehand, and while uttering his message, he may be stirred to do his best. And if that stimulus may not be derived from the congratulations of our fellows, where shall we obtain it? May it not, I ask, be supplied by the consciousness that we are "workers together" with God; that He has done us the infinite honour of asking us to co-operate with Him in the divine work of redemption; that He has summoned us from the pruning-hook and the fishing-net to co-operate with Him in bringing men from darkness to light, and from the thraldom of Satan into the kingdom of His dear Son? Surely
3

in all the world there is no dignity to be compared with that which accrues from association with such a Worker in such a work.

Such co-operation as this does not for a moment lead to indolence and lethargy. On the contrary, it stimulates us to the highest activity. You will remember how the great apostle to the Gentiles tells us that he laboured, *agonising* according to *His working* who wrought within him mightily (Col. i. 29). And, indeed, this is the natural result with all who truly realise that their fellowship is with the Father, and with His Son Jesus, and that they have been called into a divine partnership with the blessed God, travailing in birth for souls, presenting the truth as it is in Jesus, and bringing their converts through the initial difficulties which beset the entrance of the strait gate, until their faltering footsteps are firmly placed upon the way that leadeth to everlasting life.

Suppose the great artist Herkomer were to tell one of his students that he proposed to spend an entire morning helping him to finish a picture which had long been waiting on the easel for the completing touch. Can we for a moment suppose that the young novice would count the coming of the master a reason for slothful indolence ? Would it not rather be an incentive to the most careful

preparation of brush, and palette, and canvas, so
that everything might be ready to hand, and that
no single moment of precious time might be
squandered? Would he not be on the alert with
miserly care to garner every suggestion? Have
we not seen how the presence of a teacher in the
classroom has communicated the heat of his passion
to the young natures which have gathered around
him, and which have become ignited with a similar
glow? Does not the presence of the officer in the
midst of his men, so far from leading them to
lethargy, stimulate them to the highest heroism?
Surely, then, the presence of Christ, known and
felt by the preacher, should be enough to raise his
spirit to the highest degree of enthusiasm, so that
it should be pervaded by the Master's love for
men, and energised by the spirit of His untiring
devotion.

Some time ago, as I was walking along a country
road, I came on a deep saw-pit. On the edge of
the pit a sawyer stood, handling one end of a long
iron saw, the farther end of which was, of course,
hidden in the earth; but I knew that there was
another man deep in the pit, who was acting in
concert with the one I saw, and the rhythm of the
movement of whose body was in exact accordance
with that of him who stood in the spring sunlight.
The two men—one seen, the other unseen—who

were engaged on the same work, were indeed
"workers together." It struck me—and I have
often returned to the image since—that that was a
precise figure of what was intended when it was
said of our Lord that He worked together from
heaven with His disciples, as they went forth and
preached everywhere (Mark xvi. 20). [Compare
2 Cor. vi. 1.]

Throughout His life He was always working
with His apostles, and honouring them by fellowship
with Himself. The part they played was very
simple and limited; but He treated it as being
indispensable to the perfecting of His plans. He
was the root elaborating the precious juices of the
heavenly wine; but they were necessary to Him as
the branches reaching over the well, covered with
clustered fruit. And now that He is in glory, it is
by His power alone that men are regenerated and
saved; but it is for us to preach the Word, be-
lieving in His co-operating grace, and afterwards
helping those who have been impressed and con-
victed to come to the fulness of His salvation.

What a difference this makes before we enter
the pulpit! We make the passage between the
vestry and the place from which we face the
audience, whether the rostrum be fenced with
simple wooden railings or enclosed in stone,
leaning heavily upon Christ, and saying to Him,

"I will not go unless Thou go with me"; we stand before the people, more conscious of His presence than of theirs; and whilst we are preaching we keep saying in our heart, "Dear Lord, these words of mine are poor and simple, but let Thy Holy Spirit fix them as nails in a sure place." And when the sermon is over, we do not seek the flattery and commendation of men; it is enough to know that He who has summoned us to work with Him is satisfied, and that we have done that which He sent us to do.

In a Norwegian hotel the other day a little girl with one finger was strumming over a tune, the only one she knew, to the distraction of all the occupants of the room, when an accomplished pianist sat down beside her and improvised a ravishing accompaniment. After they had finished, he led the child round the company, saying, "This is the young lady whom you must thank." So may God ever accompany our poor words with the demonstration of the Holy Spirit!

VI

A DIVINE PASSION

THE other day it was my lot to hear a mission sermon. Its exegesis was correct, its illustrations apt, its spirit evidently sincere. It was altogether above the average of pulpit productions. But somehow it failed to move, because the preacher was not moved. It did not kindle, because the preacher did not glow. There was no passion in the utterance, no magnetic intensity; nothing to show that the speaker realised that he was standing between the living and the dead, and was called to plead with men as one who must give an account. And as I listened, I realised that a mirror was being held up to myself; for too often that divine passion for the souls of others has been sadly absent, and not always missed.

We are all lamenting in these days the ebb of religious interest on the part of vast masses of the people, and seek to account for it in various ways. But may we not ask whether some of the fault is not traceable to ourselves,—not that we are deficient in the traits of a consistent character; not that we are lacking in correct views of truth, or in laborious endeavour to give them a worthy representation; not that we are lazy, indolent, or careless,—but that we are deficient in passion, in enthusiasm, in glow, and intensity of spirit? We may be lights in the world, and shining lights; but there is a whole hemisphere of difference between being a shining light and a *burning* and shining light.

ILLUSTRIOUS EXAMPLES.

Allow me to recall to your minds the illustrious examples of men who have been consumed by this divine passion—of *Oliver Heywood*, who, in one year, besides his stated work on the Lord's day, preached one hundred and fifty times, kept fifty days of fasting and prayer, and nine of thanksgiving, and travelled fourteen hundred miles on horseback, in the prosecution of his laborious ministry. Of *Baxter*, whose *Reformed Pastor*, more than any other book of the same description, glows with a divine passion which all the persecutions he endured, and his excruciating physical sufferings, could not extinguish—nay, rather stirred to an intenser vehemence. Of *Whitfield*, who would spend whole days in Moorfields, at fair times, encountering the hubbub of crowds, the ridicule of

Merry Andrews, the personal violence of dastardly ruffians, the rain of stones, dirt, rotten eggs, and pieces of dead cats. Of *Wesley*, who wore out his life in labours so great, that it seemed as though he was in haste to die. Of *Brainerd*, dwelling among savages, inhabiting an ill-furnished hut in the forest, when the home of Jonathan Edwards was open to him; living on the hardest fare, praying till he was in a heavy sweat, though a cold wind was blowing, and dying in his young life, literally worn out by his labours. Or of *Dr. Payson*, who impaired his health by the frequency of his fastings and the importunity of his prayers, and of whom it is said by his biographer, that his language, his conversation, and his whole deportment were such as brought home to and fastened on the minds of his hearers the conviction that *he believed, and therefore spoke.* You may remember that he regarded it as so important to produce such an impression on the attendants of his ministry, that he announced as the topic of one of his addresses to his fellow-ministers, "The importance of convincing our hearers that we believe what we preach." And what shall I more say, for the time would fail to tell of Venn, Berridge, and Romaine; of Newton, Cecil, and Simeon; of Joseph Alleine and John Howe; of Thomas Spencer, of Liverpool, and Murray McCheyne, of Dundee,—of whom it may almost be said that the Almighty made winds His messengers, and His ministers flames of fire.

When I speak of the divine passion which should burn in our manner and words when we are handling the divine mysteries, and standing before men on the behalf of God, I want to make myself clear. I do not for a moment advocate a mere emotionalism, a continuous address to feeling, an excited and vehement series of appeals which become vapid and vain because not based on the exposition and enforcement of truth. I do not mean the suspense of the reasoning faculties or the judgment. Still less do I advocate a hysterical throwing about of the arms, contortions of the face, ranting and shouting with the voice, or foaming at the lips. I should judge that Jonathan Edwards' mighty sermon was almost entirely an appeal to the reason, and that it might be described as "logic on fire." It is not by showing the excessive signs of emotion that a speaker will beget emotions. The excessive display of our own emotion diverts the minds of our hearers from the thoughts that should excite emotion. Their observing faculties are so occupied with the gymnastic performance which is being provided for them, or they are so deafened by the roar of artillery, that they have no time to think. It is compressed steam that drives our engines. Our inspiration is not gauged by our perspiration, and we shall not arouse our audiences to go and fight Philip merely by fanning the flames of their fanaticism.

SOURCES OF THIS DIVINE PASSION.

The sources from which this divine passion is fed are various, and yet *one*.

1. In order to obtain it, we must have a purpose in each discourse we deliver. It is not enough to explain; we must enforce. We must not be content with a nice discrimination of doctrine, a statement of truth, a pretty handling of our theme, an ingenious analogy and beautiful crust of poetical sentiment. We must seek to elicit some personal, inner, and spiritual response from the consciences of our hearers. We must aim at producing revolutions; at leading up to crises in experience; at effecting some definite result in each of those whom we address. Each sermon should be inscribed with the words, "One thing I do." We must enter our pulpits or platforms intent on carrying out one point. If one method of address fails, we must try another. We knock at each door of the House of the Soul, now at the door of the Intellect, then of the Imagination, then of the Emotions. We refuse to take a denial; we must succeed, or perish in our attempt, till presently we ram our whole being into

the cannon's mouth, and discharge ourselves, for all we are worth, at the minds and hearts that have resisted minor appeals.

2. Moreover, the majesty of truth will inflame the holy passion of our souls. When the knight, in the old days of chivalry, knelt before the lady of his choice, her pure virginal presence, her stainless character, her high and noble spirit, stirred his soul to deeds of heroism, which would have been impossible apart from the glow of an intense devotion. So when the servant of God enters the Temple of Truth, and beholds the sweet and majestic presence of this earliest daughter of the Eternal, " whom He possessed in the beginning of His way, before His works of old," his soul cannot but kindle, not with sensuous passion, but with that high sentiment of reverence, of devotion, of enthralment to her service, which burns on the altar of the inner shrine with quenchless ardour.

3. The sacred fire of this divine passion is also fed by the quiet realisation of the infinite problems which are being faced day by day by the souls before us, even by those that give the slightest possible symptoms of religious earnestness. What heights of aspiration, and what depths of failure ! What hopes, and what disappointments ! What sorrows, which come near to heartbreak, crying for balm ! What mysteries crying for solution ! What

sins crying for forgiveness! If we more often substituted a consideration of the tragedy of human life as it is transacting under our eyes, not only in the glare of the great city, but in the annals of a quiet neighbourhood; if we realised the vast interests that may impinge on the delivery of a single sermon; if we entered more deeply into our Master's estimate of the value of a single soul, as the block from which an angel or a demon may be hewn, it would be impossible to be listless and insipid, icily elegant, or faultlessly correct.

"A want of earnestness," says John Angell James, "in the execution of that commission, which is designed to save immortal souls from eternal ruin, and raise them to everlasting life, is a spectacle which, if it were not common, would fill us with amazement, indignation, and contempt." We have read the speeches of the great masters of eloquence, of their intense anxiety, their untiring effort, and the mighty periods that flashed from their burning souls; and do we condemn as enthusiasts the Athenian orator who agonised to save his country from the yoke of Philip, the majestic Roman who roused the indignation of the republic against the treason of Cataline, or our own Wilberforce, who for twenty years appealed to the justice and mercy of a British Parliament against the atrocities of the slave trade? On the

contrary, we deem no eulogy sufficient to express
our admiration of their noble enthusiasm. But our
panegyric upon them is a condemnation upon ourselves; for how far short of them do we fall in
earnestness, though the salvation of a single soul,
out of all the multitudes that come under the influence of our ministrations, is an event which, in
its consequences, is inconceivably more momentous
than all the objects for which these men exhausted
the energies of their intellect and life !

When the soul is filled with this divine passion,
intent, on the one hand, on the glory of the
Redeemer, and, on the other, on the comfort, help,
and blessedness of mankind, it will insensibly
acquire all the attributes of good preaching. It
is a profound belief of mine that truth is always
allied to beauty, and that those who present her,
though in unadorned nakedness, can hardly fail to
attain to a high standard of diction and eloquence.
In reading the speeches of that consummate orator
the late John Bright, one is struck by the absence
of anything like meretricious ornament; there is
no straining for effect; the illustrations are comparatively few, and are not introduced for their
own sakes; and yet what majesty, what impressiveness in every oration !

Voltaire remarks of Cavalier that in the end
" he much failed of his first enthusiasm." It may

be that some of us are liable to the same charge. But we must remember that those who wait on the Lord *change* their strength before they mount up. They leave behind the strength of their young life, which is resourceful and self-reliant, and take instead an enduring enthusiasm which, as in the case of Christ, eats them up in self-forgetting zeal.

But there is one supreme and transcendent source of this divine passion. Our Lord said that He had come to send fire on the earth. He was the divine Prometheus who first taught the secret of a baptism of flame. Ascended to the Father's right hand, He sent forth the Divine Spirit, who descended as tongues of fire and set hearts aflame. Shall we not seek our share in that Pentecostal gift? And shall we not ask, that in the stillness of this hour we may each realise that the Fire of God has again fallen on the sacrifice, and that, after a spiritual fashion, we have again ignited our torches from the Divine Flame, as once a year they do in the Church of the Holy Sepulchre? And when the Holy Spirit has done His most effectual work, we shall not be conscious of Him, but of Jesus Christ; and each shall be able to say, with Zinzendorf, " I have but one passion: it is He, and He only."

All around the world is throbbing with passion, whether in the pursuit of trade, of science, of politics, or of pleasure; let not our congregations then feel, as they listen to our sermons on the Lord's Day and compare them with what they have encountered during the week, that they are turning from the brilliant glow of the electric light to the thin yellow flame of a small gas jet. In view of the swift movement around us, it should be impossible for any of us to preach—to make use of a coachman's phrase—" without turning a hair."

VII

SERMON CONSTRUCTION

In making a sermon, you must first be sure that you
have a definite message. It is not that you have
discovered a fantastic or striking way of treating a
text of Scripture, nor that you can bring either
poetry or learning to bear upon its treatment;
certainly not that the hour is at hand when you
must fulfil an engagement—none of these should
be the primary cause of making a sermon. You
must ask your Lord and Master to lay on you a
message from Himself.

It is always a matter of thankfulness when that
message at once associates itself with some massive
word of Scripture—a text with sea-room, which will
be a blessing to the soul that perhaps can remember
nothing of the sermon but the text—a text with far-
spreading roots to it, yet tapering to a single flower,
which offers itself for your hand to pluck and bear
to your congregation. This is why I urge the
habit of exposition on those who fulfil a regular
ministry, because necessarily they are compelled to

deal with considerable paragraphs of Scripture, even though they may announce for their text but the clause of a verse.

Take great Texts.—It is a good rule to take great texts, even though they seem deeper than any plumb-line that you possess. Their very majesty will quicken your thoughts and arouse your heart. I think, too, that we do well to keep constantly before our minds great subjects, which touch the very fundamentals of our faith, in the confident belief that the Master's message will associate itself with one of these.

When the message is obtained, and the text chosen, it is well to jot down the first thoughts that suggest themselves, in any order in which they come tumbling out of the mind. As likely as not you will not use one of them, but they will suggest others, which you will use. If you are able to leave your text or message to simmer in the sub-conscious portion of your mind for a few hours, so much the better. Go about your daily business, and whenever a thought or illustration strikes you note it down on a piece of paper, carried in a convenient pocket for the purpose. If you sleep on your subject, still so much the better. Extraordinary things are done during sleep in the laboratory of the mind. Only have your paper and pencil ready by your bed, to jot down your first waking

4

thoughts—the first pure product of *sub*-conscious, or unconscious, cerebration.

We all know the famous story of Mr. Spurgeon, who retired to rest one night, without being able to find the clue to the tangled skein of his sermon for the following day. In the morning he said to his wife, " I wish that I could only recall a treatment of my subject which presented itself in my dreams, but it is entirely gone from me." " Go to your table," was the reply, " and see what you have written there." On going across the room, he found the skeleton of a sermon on the text which had refused to yield itself to treatment on the previous night, but which had yielded its inner heart to the quiet reverie of the night. It appeared that Mrs. Spurgeon had noticed her husband arise from bed, go to the table, write down his thoughts in brief, and return to bed, apparently without awaking.

It is to compare very small things with great, to say how often I have thrown all kinds of material into the mill of my mind, to find the rags turned out as a woven tissue of paper, in which all the processes of manufacture were obliterated, and only the result remained. But this does not mean that you should be lazy all the Saturday morning and afternoon, read a number of com-mentaries over on Saturday night, and expect to find your sermon ready issued on Sunday morning. It is only when there has been honest, painstaking work that we can count on the help of the Comforter to perfect our poor work, as a great painter may go over the rude attempts of some tyro in art, removing the traces of immaturity, and leaving on the canvas the touch of a master-hand.

Study what others have said.—One of the earliest processes in sermon-building, *and only after you have jotted down all that may have occurred to your own mind*, is to consider what others have said about the theme in hand. It is only wise and right that you should read every commentary, and weigh the various renderings of the passage. If you can find sermons on the same topic, it may be perilous, but there is no harm in reading them, so long as you allow them to suggest thoughts to your own mind, whilst steadfastly refusing to transfer their paragraphs, as they stand, to your own use. There is every reason why you should study other men's thoughts, for no one supposes that your poor cranium contains the knowledge of the world, only let the thoughts which others give pass through your own mind, and, being sown in its soil, they will appear in quite another shape than that in which they were first presented to you. They will have become your own.

The Order of a Sermon.—The Introduction will probably be the last thing you will think of. When the main divisions are fixed upon, and the general drift decided, you will see in a moment what to place in your Introduction, which may recount some local circumstance or event out of which your discourse has sprung, may show the connection between your text and the context, or indicate that the message which it is on your heart to give is the natural burden of the words you have announced. It is so necessary, in your Introduction, to state clearly the lesson which you are going to enforce, and to prove that it is the legitimate voice of the passage. Often, when dealing with some historical scene, it is quite wise, with a few graphic touches, to supply the local colouring and background of the incident; but do not spend too much elaboration here.

The Divisions of your sermon must be clear and definite. There need not be *three*, there is no reason why there should not be two, or four, or more. For myself, I have a mysterious and nervous dread of *six*, which is the mark of the beast, and one less than perfection; but, with that exception, I would use indifferently each figure of the numerals.

Your divisions may not overlap. For instance, suppose a preacher, in considering the text, " Thy kingdom come," were to say, " We will consider the

kingdom of God as it is—I. Chronologically. II.
Geographically. III. Dispensationally. IV. Typi-
cally. V. Eternally." Do you not see that the
third and fourth divisions would collide? They
cover the same ground. Indeed, the phrases are
largely indentical, for, when you talk of dispensa-
tional truth, you mean that the same general
principles have reappeared under different forms
in following ages; and you are driven to treat of
David's kingdom (for instance) as foreshadowing
the reign of the Messiah; yet, what is this but to
deal with the story of the Jews as typical of things
that were to be revealed?

Suppose, also, that a preacher were to take as
his text, "Come unto Me, all ye that labour, and I
will give you rest," and should announce as his
divisions—I. The Sympathy of Christ's Call. II.
The Universality of its Appeal. III. The In-
dividuality of its Acceptance. IV. The Simplicity
of it. V. The Persons Addressed. There would
be many serious mistakes, that would greatly disturb
the success of the appeal, besides hurting the sense
of symmetry in any thoughtful persons who might
be in the audience. First, the last division really
comes in under the second, because, in dealing with
the universality of the call you naturally dwell, not
only on the word *all*, but on the fact that all men
labour and are heavy laden. Secondly, it would be

much wiser to put the sympathy (I.) and the simplicity (IV.) of the call under one head, as indicating
the characteristics of the speaker; and you might
add two or three other traits of the same kind.
Finally, the sermon-sketch might come out thus:—

I. THE CHARACTERISTICS OF THE SPEAKER—

    (a) *He is sympathetic* (tender ?).

    (b) *He is conscious of all-sufficiency in His
        person and work.*

    (c) *He is untiring* (as fresh to-day as ever).

    (d) *He is urgent* ("How shall we escape,"
        etc.—Heb. ii. 1–4).

    (e) *He is meek, and lowly in heart.*

II. THE UNIVERSALITY OF HIS APPEAL—

    (a) *All mankind are included in His in-
        carnation and propitiation.*

    (b) *The characters described are appropriate
        to every age and rank.*

    (c) *The Son of Man is above all tribal and
        racial distinctions.*

III. THE RESPONSE IT DEMANDS—

    (a) *It must be personal.*   Each for himself.

    (b) *It should be immediate.*   To-day, hear
        His voice.

    (c) *It may, in the first steps of it, be wholly
        unemotional.*   "Whosoever will."

The CLOSING APPEAL should be the most carefully prepared. What is said last will linger longest. Don't leave the closing words to haphazard. An illustration, an apt and brief incident, a verse of a familiar hymn—anything which will gather up your meaning concisely and definitely—is good. Let these closing words be delivered in a quiet, but intense, manner ; not vociferously, nor excitedly, nor with the declamation of an orator. Let them be spoken as by one who pleads with the souls of men, and in God's stead entreats them to be reconciled. Let every previous part of the sermon—its arguments, its illustrations, its quoted texts, its appeals to the emotion or fancy—and in every sermon each of these should be in evidence—conduce to the weight and impressiveness of these last words, which, delivered in co-operation with the Spirit of God, shall be like the last assault, that cannot be withstood, and before which the evil things which had proudly raised themselves against the will of God must yield, and Mansoul capitulate.

VIII

THE LEGITIMATE USE OF SCRIPTURE
IN SERMON-MAKING

IT has been one of the fundamental principles of
my ministry never to put an unnatural interpretation on Scripture, nor to use any Scripture tortuously
or unfairly. I have not heard many sermons in
the last thirty years, but I can remember a few,
in which the texts have been forced to bear an
unnatural meaning, and it seemed as though, during
the sermon, they were in torture, crying out and
protesting at the usage to which they were being
forced. This is surely what the Apostle Peter
referred to when he said that "No Scripture is
of private interpretation." Too many preachers
put their private interpretation on striking phrases
of the Word of God, and make them subserve a
meaning which the Spirit of God can hardly have
intended.

This practice is neither reverent nor wise. It
is not *reverent*; because, surely, it is more becoming
to learn what may have been the divine purpose

in any passage of Scripture than to impress it to
our own purpose. And it is not *wise*, because
thoughtful men who listen feel that the Bible can
be made to mean almost anything that its expositors
desire, and that their method of interpretation differs
widely from that to which all other books are sub-
jected. I should judge that nothing has done more
to undermine the olden faith in the Word of God
than the habit of preachers in divorcing texts from
the contexts, and making them pegs from which
to fasten ideas and exhortations which have no
more natural connection with them than a coat
with the brass hook on which it hangs. With all
my soul I protest against this use of the Bible,
and thank God that the influence of my sainted
and beloved friend, Rev. C. M. Birrell, has always
made it an impossibility for myself.

Shakespeare says that the devil can quote
Scripture to his purpose, and you will remember
that on the one occasion when he quoted it to
Christ, he so divorced an injunction from its
associated verses that our Lord had to correct
him by saying, "It is written again." A great
many of the difficulties, which trouble people
concerning certain statements in the Scripture,
would disappear if only they would carefully read
the whole paragraph or book of which they form
a part, and explain the part by the whole.

It would be possible to prove every assertion of the agnostic or materialistic philosophy of the present day by isolated passages culled from the Book of Ecclesiastes. It is absolutely essential in the case of that book to read it from end to end, when at once one discovers that it is a satire on life spent "under the sun," without reference to the unseen or eternal realities for which the heart of man was made. And there are isolated texts, or fragments of texts, in the Epistle to the Hebrews which appear full of condemnation to the soul that has taken one backward step, until the whole treatise is read from end to end, when it is seen that the writer is endeavouring to show that Christianity is the supreme message of God, which can have no sequel, and that therefore to reject it is to throw away the only rope that hangs over the face of the precipice, and to refuse the one boat that lies on the desolate shore of time.

These two instances are sufficient to prove my point. But I remember a further illustration of a preacher who announced as his text the words, "I will say to the north, Give up; and to the south, Keep not back." The north, in his sermon, stood for evil companions and unholy associates; whilst the south stood for the public-house, the house of shame, and such like haunts of evil. It was, no doubt, a striking sermon, but I gravely question whether he could not have found other texts which would have served his purpose better than in wresting the Scripture in this way.

Our main end in preaching is not to bring our thoughts to the Bible, but to bring out God's thoughts before the gaze of our fellows. This habit will demand more thoughtful attention, care, and time, but it will have its abundant compensations. It will afford an unfailing well-spring of interest; it will keep the speaker fresh and interesting; it will attract thoughtful people who love the Word of God; and it will enable the Spirit of God to wield His own sword with unfailing effect. Nothing so absolutely overcomes the resistance of the sinner as to be met with, "Thus saith the Lord."

When a text strikes you, be sure to put it down instantly in your memorandum book with the thoughts that gather freshly around it. It is most important to do this. You may imagine that you will recall them, but it is as impossible to do so as to describe the hues of sunset after they have faded. Then at your leisure open to the passage, read the entire paragraph, especially as it is given in the Revised Version. See if it will naturally bear the use that you are disposed to make of it. If not, dare to refuse to use the text in that sense, and wait until you can deduce the same lesson obviously and naturally from some other passage. It is well, also, to turn to the original, or if it be in the Epistles, to Conybeare's and Howson's translation of St. Paul's Epistles, or to some first-rate commentary, that with the help of other minds you may be able to determine the fundamental meaning and drift of the context.

I referred in my last paper to the right methods of expository preaching. But let it be remembered that he is an expositor who carefully weaves the context into the sermon, which he delivers on some pivot text, quite as much as he is who, Sunday after Sunday, pursues his way through some entire book of Scripture. In this sense Dr. M'Laren is a true expositor, for though he rarely goes through an entire book consecutively, yet he never takes a subject without showing how naturally it arises, not only from the text, but also from the context.

But always recollect that you are not warranted in preaching to others that which you have not made a matter of your personal religious consciousness. Nothing so injures us as to preach beyond our own experiences and aims.

IX

EXPOSITORY PREACHING

I HAVE already touched on this matter in the previous pages, but its importance demands that some further words be said on it, though perhaps they are more pertinent to those who address the same stated audience than to the temporary supply or the local preacher.

It has been the almost invariable rule of Presbyterian ministers to expound books of Scripture in regular course at one or both of the services on each recurring Lord's day. And from them the habit has been passed on to many of our strongest preachers, the freshness and resourcefulness of whose pulpit instruction have held large congregations through long pastorates. As I write, I recall two remarkable examples of this practice—men whom I knew and admired, each of whom is now with God—Hugh Stowell Brown of Liverpool, W. M. Taylor of New York; and with these may be classed Dr. Dale of Birmingham, whose preaching was largely formed on this model.

There are two methods of preaching which are far as the poles asunder, the *topical* and the *expository*. In the former the preacher selects as his theme some subject in theology or philosophy, or some topic suggested by the current life and table talk of the day, makes his address, and then looks into his Bible or concordance for an appropriate motto-text, more or less suitable, but there is perhaps the smallest possible connection between the discourse and the text. In the latter the preacher prayerfully selects some extended tract of Scripture on which he proposes to concentrate himself for a considerable term of services; carefully breaks it up into paragraphs, each of which will probably yield him at least one sermon; studies the whole to get the general tenor, and then concentrates himself on each separate part, with the result that his soul is dyed with the message that burdened the prophet or evangelist who spoke, centuries ago, in the power of the Holy Spirit. The former method needs a much cleverer man; the latter will enable a man of very moderate abilities to fulfil a long and useful pastorate which will make his people Bible students, acquainted with the whole range of Scripture truth, and less liable than most to be swept away by every wind of doctrine and sleight of cunning craftiness.

It may be objected that people will weary of this

kind of preaching. If they do, it is because of some mistake in the method by which the preacher sets to his work. Of course, if he persists in the microscopic examination of every verse as the Puritan Caryl on the Book of Job, who, I believe, devoted seven years to his painstaking toil, he may, like his illustrious predecessor, begin with a crowd and end with an audience of seven persons, *faint, yet pursuing.* In his biography of my predecessor in the pastorate at Surrey Chapel and Christ Church, Dr. Allon relates that the Rev. James Sherman confessed to have made a mistake in expounding the Psalms in a series of sermons, through a succession of years, because there was necessarily so much sameness in the theme and his treatment. But these cases, whilst serving to show where the rocks lie, need not dissuade us from launching on the broad bosom of the noble current of Bible exposition. We must see to it that our course of sermons should not last for more than six or seven months, unless, as is generally the case, we find the interest deepening and widening to such an extent that we feel justified in pursuing a leisurely course. An epistle need not take more than that time, while a gospel may demand a year and more.

The *wrong* method of expository preaching is to give out ten or a dozen verses as your text, which has the immediate effect of depressing your hearers,

who naturally wonder how long it will take you to
treat so many verses when so short a text as " *Jesus
wept* " will occupy you at least forty minutes. The
children, whose parents expect them to write out
or learn the text, are naturally the most depressed
of all. It is a bad start, but the bad is made worse
if the unlucky preacher goes on to say, " I propose
to make a few remarks on this passage." Oh, those
few remarks ! First, they are not likely to be
few ; second, they show that he has probably not
studied his subject, and is simply hoping to get a
start from one of the verses, and that if he is persecuted in one, he will flee to another ; and, third,
he is likely, like a dishonest milkman, to add so
much water to the sincere milk of the Word that
his audience will become as attenuated as children
who are fed on skimmed milk.

The *right* method of exposition is to discover the
pivot verse, on which the whole paragraph revolves,
and in which it centres. That is likely enough to
burn itself into your heart as the message of the
Lord, like the focal point of a burning lens. You will
then find that you can draw upon the whole passage
for the elucidation or enforcement of this one brief
sentence. Every clause falls into its place and
order, so that you have no lack of forceful material
for the elaboration of your theme. Of course, you
announce *this* as your text. If there are strangers

present, they do not feel as though they must suffer loss by reason of having missed the former sermons; the discourse appeals to them as a completed picture; and perhaps only your own people are aware that it is part of a series. In my judgment, it is even a mistake to spend too much time in recapitulation; it is much better to plunge at once into the statement of the theme which your text has suggested, and to open up, as you should always do in your introduction, the method of treatment which you intend to pursue.

The advantages of this habit are threefold.

First. Your people will be kept in constant contact with the Word of the living God.

Second. They will be interested to come again and again to pursue the line of teaching which has blessed or helped them, as people will buy the magazine in which the serial story ends with the words, *To be continued in our next.*

Third. You will be led to consider passages of the Word of God which your own temperament or habit of thought might lead you to avoid, and which might seem so pertinent to the case of people in your audience that you might be accused of being too personal. But these objections do not hold when the passage which is so peculiarly appropriate comes in the regular order of exposition. I have found again and again that nothing has so pulled

5

up a flagging congregation, or retained a full one, **as a** series of expositions; and if I may refer to my **own books,** they have all come into existence in this way.

Let me give one caution. Though you shall carefully study every authority in your reach, and especially the original Hebrew or Greek, it is not wise to needlessly obtrude the names of your authorities or your knowledge of the original languages on your audience. Give your people the results, and do not worry them with the process. It is enough for the bees to give us honey; you know in a moment if the amalgam is right. It is not necessary for our tiny purveyors to tell us how far they flew over the clover fields, and what were the names of the flowers from which they gathered their precious and appetising stores.

> " Then bless thy secret growth, nor catch
>   At noise, but strive unseen and dumb ;
> Keep clean, bear fruit, earn life, and watch,
>   Till the white-winged reapers come."

X

A GREAT SERMON

THE greatest sermon ever preached since the re-
surrection of our Lord was that of the day of
Pentecost, the notes of which are recorded for our
instruction, not only as to the *matter*, but the
manner. Few things are more helpful to a young
preacher than to take up the masterpieces of pulpit
eloquence, with which literature abounds, to analyse
them, and to try and discover their salient characteristics. We may learn all we need to know of
the art of pulpit eloquence by studying the sermons
of a M'Laren, Spurgeon, or Phillips Brooks—each
of which stands for a distinct method. How much
more, then, may we learn by a careful study of this
great sermon, which inaugurated the movement of
which the Christianity of to-day is the lasting
memorial ?

1. In glancing down that sermon we are arrested
first by the fact that it consists so largely of quotation. Out of twenty-two verses, ten at least are
given up to the quotation of Scripture from the

Old Testament. This well deserves attention. Modern sermons are not sufficiently filled with the Word of God.

It is the custom of some well-known preachers, who have always secured a wide and intelligent audience, to quote various corroborative passages from the Bible, accustoming their hearers to turn from verse to verse in their company. I cannot but feel that this is a most instructive way of preaching, and it is much better to read the Word of God with your people than misquote it. This habit serves to keep your congregation on the alert. The rustle of leaves is very significant of their painstaking interest and desire to search the Word of God, and the result is a ready acquaintance with all parts of Scripture, which is of the utmost service in establishing Christian people in the faith. I have tried this system now and again with good results, but somehow it does not well suit my idiosyncrasy. I admire the custom and advocate it for others, and if I were beginning again I think I would endeavour to make this a facile habit of my pulpit. It certainly is my custom in Bible readings, but in preaching I find that the constant turning of the pages of the Bible checks me in the flow of my thought and the cumulative effect of my address.

Perhaps some of us can secure the same result

by saturating our sermons with the spirit of Scripture, and by quoting from memory certain apposite passages. This is a special characteristic of Dr. M'Laren, most of the telling points of whose sermons are clinched by so apt a quotation of Scripture as to flood it with a ray of illuminating glory. I would specially urge young preachers to fill their sermons with the Word of God, which is the sword of the Spirit. Let the Spirit have something in your discourses on which He may lay hold. It is interesting to read the sermons of James Parsons, some of which seem to be little else than a mosaic of Scripture texts; and probably in his generation there was no one more eminently used than he was to the conversion of men. You may be sure that, since all Scripture is profitable for teaching, for reproof, for correction, and for instruction, the more there is of it in your sermons the better.

2. Glancing down this sermon one notices also the apostle's reference to events and objects which were within the knowledge of his audience. Notice specially the 22nd verse, " Wonders and signs which God did by Him *in the midst of you*, even as ye yourselves know," and 29th verse, " His tomb is with us unto this day." In too many sermons there is an aloofness from the ordinary thought and life of our people which is very prejudicial to our

success. *We* have been in our studies and amongst our books, whilst *they* have been immersed in business care and anxiety, and if we want to arrest and hold them, we must learn the sacred art of leading them from the things with which they are most familiar to the unseen and eternal; and the transition should be as easy and natural as possible.

In the works of Charles Dickens one is perpetually arrested by his habit of leading the attention forward by almost insensible degrees. If he is describing a house, he conducts you from the road where you are standing to the gate, describes the gate, and the little path that leads to the door, whether paved with bricks or chips. He tells you whether the door is open or shut, and what creeper has climbed along the trellis-work. In this way you are conducted into the midst of scenes transacting within the house, of which you need to know. And you may be sure that he will be the successful preacher, whether to children or adults, who can enchain their interest, and lead from the familiar to the less familiar, and from the seen to the unseen. Do not scruple, then, to allude to " the tomb of David," which is within the knowledge of all your people; and remember how our Lord spoke of the commonest, simplest incidents by which His daily life was surrounded, showing the close connection between the natural and the supernatural.

3. The apostle constantly appeals to personal experience. Verse 32, "Whereof we all are witnesses." The personal element entered very largely into the sermons in the Acts of the Apostles. Please turn to them for the further corroboration of this remark. There is a great difference between the egotistic reference to oneself and the simple testimony of witness-bearing which has for its aim the exaltation of the Lord. There are times in the history of every preacher when he has a right to exclaim with the beloved apostle, "Things which I have tasted, seen, and handled, concerning the Word of Life, I announce."

4. Again, there was great directness in this sermon. Preached as it was in the power of the Holy Spirit, and burning throughout with His sacred fire, it was evidently a message from God, but it was equally a message to men. Verse 22, "*Ye* men of Israel." "*Ye* yourselves." Verse 23, "*Ye* . . . did crucify." Verse 36, "This Jesus whom *ye* crucified." Oh for the power to charge home men's sins upon their hearts! There must be a directness in our addresses. Each sermon must say in the words of Nathan, "Thou art the man." We must cultivate the habit of particular preaching. We must prepare and preach our sermons with reference to distinct types of character and experience. What is aimed at nothing can hit nothing.

Have a purpose, an objective, a personal reference in your heart when you stand up to preach, and if you are conscious of having one hand in the grip of Christ, do not scruple with the other hand to strike directly at the heart of man.

5. Lastly, there was much prayer before the sermon; in this case ten days. The fleece must lie out in the dark night before it can be saturated with dew; and unless it is so drenched, it will be impossible to wring out from it a bowl of water. I like the story of the poor local preacher, suddenly called upon to preach in a big chapel. He kept saying, " I dursen't do it." Presently he was forced into the pulpit, and the door shut on him; and he fell on his knees, with bowed head. Presently he was heard to say, " Aye, Maister, I've seen *Thee*; I can manage it now."

XI

MY OWN METHOD

THE question has often been put to me, "What is your own method of sermon-making?" I shrink a little from complying with the request to tell, because it might suggest that I was a sermon-maker of so notable a kind that it would be well worth the while of others to copy my example, whereas I am very conscious of not having attained "to the first three." I am a servant to whom the Lord gave two talents—the lad with five barley loaves and two small fish. Besides this, it is a mistake for men at the beginning of their ministerial preaching career to imitate the methods of a man who, for thirty-five years, has been preaching never less than three, and often as many as eight or nine, sermons a week. Necessarily one's method has greatly altered, as practice and experience have given one facilities which were not possible in the earlier days.

I fear my style was but a ragged one when in 1869–70 I settled as assistant minister at

Pembroke Chapel, Liverpool.   There I came in
contact with the chaste and exquisite style of the
Rev. C. M. Birrell, who was accustomed to write
and commit to memory every sermon; and in
imitation of him, which was the sincerest flattery,
I, too, set to work to write and learn every word.
This practice I continued for about fifteen years.

As for the writing, I may fairly say that I owe
to this habit more advantage than I can possibly
express.   It had two results.   First, it compelled
me to think carefully through the subject.   My
pen was the bond that kept my thoughts steadily
concentrated upon the theme with which I was
dealing, and in due time it became possible for me
to fix my mind with all the power of which it was
capable in prosecuting in various directions one
subject of sacred meditation.   This habit has been
invaluable to me in the somewhat broken life
which I have been compelled to follow in subsequent years, and at almost any moment, when it
is necessary, I can concentrate my mind upon some
subject, undisturbed by the rush of the railway
train, the tumult of a station, or the incidents of a
tramway ride through the crowded streets of the
metropolis.   Secondly, I ascribe to this habit any
lucidity or transparency of style of which my pen
is possessed.

In writing my sermons during these years, I was

in the habit of mercilessly tearing up page after page if I was not satisfied. Often I would spend three or four hours in writing my introduction. It appeared as if I was possessed by the spirit of fastidiousness, and unless my expressions seemed exactly suitable and adequate, I was not content to let them pass, and instead of merely erasing them and substituting others, I was not satisfied unless the page on which I wrote was clear and clean. I had little idea of what was being secured by these wasted sheets of closely written paper. In those days I had not as yet written a page for printing. I had no idea that people would care to read what I wrote. I was preserved from the temptation to expend myself unduly in the service of the reading public. Enclosed within the walls of my study, uninvaded in those days by a constant succession of visitors, like a coral island within its reef, I was able to grow flowers and fruit which, without doubt, have enriched my style and teaching in all after days. I am quite sure that I could never have stood the subsequent constant drain upon my resources had it not been for those blessed, placid, pellucid years of quiet work.

In later years, during my ministry in London, I have not been able to write, but the habits of consecutive thinking and clear expression, which were formed at York and Leicester, have stood me in good stead. It is now my ideal to select my text fairly early in the week, and allow it to lie in my thought. Then, on Friday or Saturday, I will give three or four hours to its quiet consideration, jotting down thoughts which occur to me on sheets of note-paper, and reading whatever materials I may have in my library that will help me. I greatly enjoy this accumulation of my materials. After a while the main message of the sermon becomes apparent. One feels that this is the burden of the Lord for the coming service. The argument, the illustrations, the application, all stand out, and it is comparatively easy in an hour or less to crystallise the whole preparation into the outline of the sermon. I have known cases in which that outline did not appear clearly until within an hour or two of preaching, but when that is the case, it does not greatly concern me. One comes to trust a species of automatic process by which the mind will ultimately evolve the message and its ordering. Often during those hours of preparation, whilst engaged with the accumulation of material or in its orderly arrangement, the heart is lifted up for the enlightenment of God's Spirit, on which one may surely count, if one has no object other than to be the message-bearer of the Lord of Hosts.

I notice that many ministers spend a great deal of time in finding striking headings for the divisions of their subject. I think too much can be made of these. I have sometimes noticed that the appetising names on a French menu or bill of fare have been disappointing, because the viands have not been equal to the expectations excited; and in some sermons I have felt that the divisions and the headings promised more than the subsequent paragraphs supplied. By all means get good and striking headings for your subdivisions, but do not be content with these; let them be subsidiary to the main body of your teaching. Get the subject matter of your paragraphs first, and label them afterwards.

Above all things, spare neither time nor pains in obtaining an orderly arrangement of your subject, so that you may not repeat yourself, or introduce into one part of your sermon matter extraneous to its main drift. But of this we will treat with more care presently.

Meanwhile, repeat often to yourself those words of Coventry Patmore, of the man after God's own heart—

> " Nor can he quail
>   In faith, nor flush, nor pale
> When all the other idiot people spell
> How this or that new prophet's word belies
>   Their last high oracle ;
>   But constantly his soul
>   Points to its pole
> E'en as the needle points, and knows not **why**."

XII

ON THE USE OF OTHER MEN'S THOUGHTS

THERE is a regular and systematic use of other men's thoughts, which should always be going on, and without which our own mind will soon become barren and unproductive. In his *Ascent of Man*, Professor Drummond quotes an interesting observation from the pages of Herodotus. When he was in Egypt, this close observer of men and manners noticed that at a certain season of the year the Egyptians went into the desert, cut off branches from the wild palms, and bringing them back to their gardens, waved them over the flowers of the date palm. Why they performed this ceremony they did not know, but they knew that if they neglected it the date crop would be poor or wholly lost. The true reason is now explained. The garden plants which bore the dates were the feminine, whilst the desert palms were masculine, and the waving of the wild branches meant the transference of the pollen dust from one to the other. Similarly we need the infusion of the thoughts of others to make our minds productive. It is not that we are to give them forth as we receive them, but that they shall stir our own minds to independent action, the joint product being different to what either mind would have elaborated from itself.

This is the true method of using other men's thoughts. Always have in reading one or more thoughtful and thought-breeding books. If they are of a different school of thinking or order of mind from your own, so much the better. Read slowly; consider, ponder, criticise, and even antagonise what you read; have your notebook ready to jot down your first fresh impressions. I fear I have, comparatively speaking, read but few books, but a really strong book occupies me for so long from my habit of mind in reflecting a good deal on what I read.

If you are going to preach to the same people for a succession of years—perhaps we might also say of months—you must enrich the soil of your mind and heart by taking in the suggestions and conclusions of other thinkers. The farmer will tell you that if he doesn't put into his land as much as he takes out, it will soon become unproductive. The method of agriculture just now in vogue is specially insistant on the incessant and scientific enrichment of the soil. And the same law is operant with all who are perpetually raising crops of holy and helpful sermons, addresses, and books.

Beware of always reading theological works. They may be the easiest to master and assimilate, but they will not stir your mind so much as those which, because they lie somewhat outside your province, will arouse and task you more. Besides, you should be ever on the alert to get new view-points for the subjects you wish to unfold, new methods of approach to your hearers, and new illustrations; these you are much more likely to obtain in works on philosophy, mental science, and physical research. I never can forget the mental stimulus which I obtained from Mill's two volumes on *Logic and the Laws of Thought*, never knowing which to admire more, the lucidity of his thought, his mastery over its expression, or the appropriate illustrations with which he made his meaning perfectly clear.

Volumes of history, travel, exploration, and biography will yield handfuls of illustrations, which should be carefully garnered, transferred to the pages of the commonplace book, and indexed in such a manner as to be easily recalled when their appropriate subject comes next to be considered. There is nothing more important than to know how to be able to lay one's hands on one's materials.

We may have piles of suitable illustrations, incidents, and poetry, but if we cannot recall them when we need, of what use are they? One of the best methods I know, when the books you have been reading belong to you, is to note in the margin of a Bible kept for the purpose the place where you may find some suitable illustration or remark, or do the same on a page of your note-book. This habit continued over a course of years will give you a clue to the elucidation and lighting-up of many hundreds of passages.

Whatever you do, don't be always reading other men's sermons. These most easily and insensibly lead us on to plagiarism. Suppose one, for instance, should read that glorious sermon of Phillips Brooks on "The Egyptians dead upon the Seashore," or that sublime sermon of Mr. Spurgeon on "Deep calling to deep"—it would be impossible not to wish to preach on the same text, but it would be almost impossible to do so without falling into their lines of thought. On the whole, it is better to read the books out of which sermons can be made and are being made.

It does not seem to me necessary to load your address with the names of your authors, except you give their exact words. The practice, doubtless, gives your hearers an impression of your wide reading and research; but since you do not go to the

6

pulpit to magnify yourself, the less there is of this the better. It is not necessary, either, to explain all the steps that have led you to certain con- clusions. Give your people bread of winnowed corn ; they will appreciate and thank you for it ; but it is not needful to explain the processes through which it has passed, or the markets from which you procured it.

The one point on which it is impossible to insist too much is that you thoroughly assimilate what other men have supplied. As the digestion of the mother assimilates every variety of food and passes it on in the form of pure, rich milk to the hungry lips of her child, so should we take into ourselves that which afterwards we are to impart to others. Too often in his quotations the preacher flings at his audience undigested material which is not of the same substance as the remainder of his dis- course, and therefore rather hinders than helps the entire effect.

I find that it is almost imperative to allow some time to elapse between the accumulation of material and the actual preparation of the sermon, that the process of mental digestion may be allowed to do the work. A day or two days are not too much, and by all means include a night. I greatly believe in unconscious cerebration, which is another name for mental digestion. At night I have found most wonderful results achieved whilst I slept. If your material is in an undigested, disorderly shape when you retire to rest, you will on awaking, as likely as not, find that the tangled skein will run as smooth as if it had been touched by a fairy wand.

Whatever you do, don't be a plagiarist. "Thou shalt not steal" applies to sermons as well as to coins of money. Remember that the habit will grow on you, so that soon you will have lost all faculty for original production. In any case, when you are giving another man's sermon, hold up two fingers of your right hand as you begin and two fingers of your left as you close, showing that all between is *in quotation marks!*

When we begin to pilfer others' thoughts, and transfer them as they stand into the fabric of our sermons, we are sewing new cloth on an old garment; most people can see the joining, and there will be some tearing sooner or later.

XIII

ON YOUR DELIVERY

THE best matter in the world will be ineffective if the method of delivery is poor and halting; and it seems wise, therefore, to give a few hints as to the best way of giving utterance to your message, so that your manner may not hinder the thoughtful and reverent reception of your matter.

Stand naturally before the people. Do not stand on one foot, but on both. Do not loll or lean on the pulpit or desk, but stand quietly in front of it. Do not run, walk, or move from side to side; and if you step back for a moment, return as soon as possible to your former position. Some preachers remind one of caged animals, who are always pacing to and fro, contending with the bars of their cage, and producing in the spectators the weary sense of restlessness. This is not well, and should be altered. Who, that ever heard, John Bright, Mr. Gladstone, or Mr. Spurgeon, can remember any such excessive activity? This habit distracts the attention of the audience, and has nothing to commend it.

Look at your hearers. The eye possesses a wonderful power of fascination. It speaks; it fixes the attention of your congregation; it interprets to the speaker, instinctively and immediately, the emotions which his words are exciting. Open eye meets eye; and by the glance the thought is kindled, and kindles the soul. Don't look up, as though to look where angels are must necessarily give you an angelic expression. Don't look down, as though you were ashamed. Don't look into far-away space, or your features will become expressionless. Look at your people honestly, manfully, straightforwardly, and glance from one to another naturally. I am not at all sure that I admire that far-away look in the eyes, in which I am told that some ministers excel.

Speak naturally. You can fill the largest building, with a very thin voice, if you observe these three conditions—speak deliberately, articulate distinctly, especially the final consonants, and let your voice come as far as possible from the chest. A little practice will enable you to bring your voice down from the throat to the chest, and the notes which the chest gives are much deeper, more reverberant, and more touching than any others.

Whatever you do, don't cultivate a pulpit voice, which is wholly detestable; don't imitate another preacher, however famous; and don't play always on one poor note. How well I remember Mr.

Spurgeon speaking to us students, years ago, on this bad practice and parodying a hymn—

> "Strange that a harp of a thousand strings
> Should play one note so long."

Who ever heard of a lawyer suffering from a lawyer's throat, or a barrister from a barrister's throat ? Men in other professions are perpetually using their voices as continuously as ministers and preachers do, but no ill effects follow. And they would not follow in our own case if we spoke naturally, using the entire range of our voice, and allowing our hearers the infinite relief of variety. I have often noticed the quiet which has fallen upon my audience when I have suddenly awoke to realise that I had been speaking too much in one key, and have suddenly fallen or risen to another. Their ears, nerves, and brains have blessed me.

Do not shout or bawl ; it is most objectionable, and absolutely unnecessary. Perspiration is not inspiration. God was not in the thunder, but in the still, small voice. When Jesus taught the people, He opened His mouth and breathed to the bottom of His lungs the good fresh air, but He would speak in the soft, sweet tones that befitted His enumeration of Beatitudes and His call to rest. On the other hand, don't whisper or drop your voice, or begin so low that people must strain to hear you. These are mannerisms and affectations which will greatly detract from the effect of your preaching.

Guard against eccentricity. Whatever attracts the attention of your hearers from your message to yourself is a mistake. Don't run your hand through your hair, though I believe geniuses have been known to do it. Don't shake or nod your head, though it gives the impression of sententiousness. Don't play with a button of your waistcoat, or put your hands in your pockets. Don't flash a gold ring in the light. Be ashamed of yourself and confess your sin if you strike the attitude that best sets off your figure. Get your wife to imitate your peculiarities of delivery when you get home, especially when you feel that you have preached well. You will be shocked at what you have done; or, if you haven't a wife, get some fatherly old deacon to hold a mirror up to nature, so that you may see yourself as others see you. Ah, how I have suffered from these loving hints, and how they have cauterised my soul !—but I would not have been without them for a good deal.

Avoid excessive gesticulation. By all means let there be some movement of the hands and face, and of the position of the body. But these should not be excessive. It is a mistake to lift the hands above the head or far above the level of the shoulder. It is equally a mistake to swing them round like the sails of a windmill, or fling them backwards and forwards like a flail. They may hang by your side, or rest on the book-board or rail, or be extended in entreaty, or raised in warning, or one of them may be used to strengthen the point you are enforcing, with a confirmatory gesture. But don't pound at the Bible, or strike the balustrade or railing, or wring your hands in agony, or perform with them the act which you are describing. Power will be ours if we wait quietly in the presence of God until we have been endued with power from on high. "Not by might, nor by power, but by My Spirit, saith the Lord."

I have often thought of the old rhyme which has come down through two or three generations of preachers—

> "Begin low, proceed slow ;
> Rise higher, take fire ;
> When most impressed, be self-possessed."

Some men have naturally an easy, unaffected address, others suffer from a diffidence, which creates mannerism and awkwardness. It is, of course, best to think as little as possible about our peculiarities, lest we lessen the simplicity and directness of our message. At the same time, we should endeavour to prune away eccentricities and remove blemishes, that we may become as panes of clear glass through which the light of the gospel may, as easily as possible, visit those that sit in darkness and the shadow of death.

XIV

THE USE OF ILLUSTRATION

OTHER things being equal, the preacher who uses
illustrations will be surest of an audience and of
the intelligent appreciation of his hearers; for the
effort to employ them indicates a desire on his part
to accommodate himself to the capacity of the
people, and to translate divine truth into human
experience and life.

No man ever spake as our Lord did, because none
has been so prolific as He in the use of illustration.
Sometimes it must have seemed that His discourses
were a tesselated work of parables and metaphors.
He was constantly introducing the most exquisite
vignettes of human life with the words "The kingdom of heaven is like." And a careful study of His
method would greatly enrich and enhance our power
of presenting truth to the minds of men.

To some the readiness to trace spiritual laws and
analogies in the natural world, and to find "sermons
in stones, and books in the running brooks," is more
easy than with others; but with all, the habit is

capable of cultivation and training. And a few suggestions may be made which will be of service in the formation and education of this most necessary branch of the preacher's art.

1. *We should be always on the alert to note facts which give promise of serving as illustrations.* The wider your range of study and observation, the more fertile and prolific will be your opportunity of gathering illustrations. There are, first, the illustrations borrowed from the incidents of domestic and ordinary life—the child asking bread of its father, the patching of old garments, the use of old bottle-skins, the careful hen gathering the chicks under her wing, the lamp put on the lampstand, the leaven buried in the flour, the birds that have neither store-house nor barn, the foxes that creep to their holes, the flowers that neither toil nor spin.

Next, there are the illustrations afforded by the closer study of nature. For these we should either adopt some branch of natural investigation as our hobby, or should study some weekly paper, like *Nature*, which is devoted to natural research. A Russian friend of mine, who is an enthusiastic student of nature, is constantly writing articles which obtain a vast circulation among persons of widely differing theological and ecclesiastical views, because she uses the most recent discoveries as the vehicle of elucidating and enforcing the lessons of the divine life in the soul. Dr. Hugh MacMillan has laid us all under obligation for his work on similar lines.

Beside these, there are the illustrations borrowed from the arts, from processes of manufacture, and from scientific discovery—as the figure of Laocoon and his sons encircled by the serpent folds, to illustrate the clinging power of evil; as the manufacture of steel, to illustrate the varying discipline to which God exposes His saints; as the uplifted hand of the electric car grasping the overhead wire, to illustrate the abiding of the believer in union with the power of God; as the invention of wireless telegraphy, to illustrate the power of prayer.

No man who desires a fund of fresh and vivid illustration can afford to dispense with the daily newspaper, reflecting as it does the life of the world around. What forcible and apt illustrations Mr. Moody used to draw from the American War; and of late the descriptions sent home from the field of war have furnished us with a vast store of words and incidents which have served us well, because they were already in our hearers' minds. I believe it was said of the late Dr. Brock that he regarded his morning study of the *Times* as a sacred duty, that his preaching might keep in touch with the life around him.

Besides these sources, there is the almost infinite

storehouse of literature. A thorough knowledge of Shakespeare, of Charles Dickens, and of Walter Scott will amply repay the preacher, replete as they are with types of character, with graphic and pathetic incidents, and with touches of natural beauty. I mention these as specimens of many others—such as the works of Stevenson, Barrie, Ian Maclaren, Shorthouse, etc.

But from whatever source you seek these goodly pearls, you must be careful to have your notebook always in hand to fix the fact, and the lesson it suggests, on the spot. The thought, the analogy, the comparison, flashes before the mind for a moment, brief as the rush of the meteor; you see and appreciate it; you say to yourself, "I shall certainly not fail to recall that idea when I need it"; but it is a hundred chances to one that it will elude you, and mock all your efforts at recovery. The only method of retaining these fugitive impressions is to note them down by one or two characteristic phrases which will summon the whole scene to your mind when you presently sit down to elaborate the illustration under the appropriate heading of your commonplace book. This bears the same relation to the pocket notebook as the ledger does to the day-book.

The illustrations must be fairly familiar. It is a mistake to use those which are wholly foreign to the life of the people whom you address. There was a touch of nature in the advice of Mr. Spurgeon that we should not employ images which savour of the special calling of the people whom we are addressing, lest they discover some minor inaccuracy in our metaphor, and therefore justify themselves in refusing the truth which was wrapt up in it. He said that it was not wise for the average preacher to talk to fisherfolk about fishing, or to husbandmen about agriculture; but to change about and use the talk of the fields for the fishers, and the talk of the fish for the peasants. But, for all that, we are wise, on the whole, to draw our illustrations from the familiar environment of our hearers.

Nothing can be more foreign to your purpose than to use illustrations which need as much explanation as the truth you are inculcating; for you divert the minds of your hearers from the truth to an honest attempt to understand your analogy. This is as disappointing as the story of the good soul who said that she understood Bunyan's *Pilgrim's Progress*, and was hoping in due time to understand the explanatory notes also.

The object in using illustrations is to bring the unseen and eternal within the range of ordinary minds, and to express the things of the spiritual world in the language of the senses and the soul. It is easier for ordinary people to think of the concrete than of the abstract, of the image than the spiritual counterpart, of the sign than the thing signified; therefore we use illustrations as the ladder by which they may climb; but the foot of the ladder must be on the spot of ground on which they happen to have lighted.

The illustrations must really add to the growing effect of the argument. Preachers sometimes introduce most picturesque descriptions with no other object, so far as one can see, than to attract attention to their delicacy and beauty. Such illustrations resemble the pictures hung on the walls of your chamber, rather than the windows through which light enters. The result is that the fancy is entranced with the chaste beauty which lights up the discourse, but the mind returns with an effort to the main current of thought. The streamlet we explored was very lovely, but we find that we have wasted strength in exploring it which might have been better expended on the navigation of the main channel.

This always seemed to me to be the defect of the late Dr. Guthrie's sermons. They abound with word-pictures of extraordinary brilliance and eloquence. One feels that he must have expended superabundant toil and pains on elaborating them, but somehow they do not add to the strength of his sermons. One lingers to gaze on them with such interest as to forget that they were intended to teach or enforce. To borrow the phrase which Dr. William Taylor quotes from a cabinetmaker, we may ornament construction, but have no right to construct ornament.

Illustrations should follow, and not precede, the thoughtful presentation of truth. If we always hasten to present a striking illustration to our hearers, we shall do them the permanent injury of weakening their powers of reasoning and apprehension. Our people should be trained to think, to base their beliefs on scriptural authority, to apprehend statements of truth in their unadorned beauty and simplicity. But when this has been done, it is highly beneficial to employ illustrations to confirm and clinch the impression, to elucidate it for those to whom it may not be quite clear, and to call in the aid of the imagination to assist the memory in her office.

Nothing is more befitting than to argue your way up some steep and difficult ascent, suiting your pace to that of your hearers, and assured that they are accompanying you, till you bring them to an angle on the steep mountain path from which, in an instant, the whole panorama towards which you have been making your way bursts on their view in an apt illustration.

When the preacher has but one aim in view, viz. to glorify the Lord Jesus by the enunciation of

His truth, it is wonderful to find how the whole mind is aroused and enriched. When the eye is single, the whole body is full of light. Thoughts, arguments, proof-texts, illustrations, and metaphors come readily at our call; and it is as though the promise were being fulfilled: "Seek ye first the kingdom of God, and all these things shall be added unto you." If you preach your sermons simply to dazzle and interest people by the introduction of gleams of imagination and bits of word-painting, you will find them fail you. But if you have only one desire and purpose—the glory of your King—the Holy Spirit will marvellously quicken the action of your mind, and will endow you with a surprising fertility of apposite and striking illustration.

> " There is a shrine whose golden gate
>   Was opened by the hand of God ;
>   It stands serene, inviolate,
>   Though millions have its pavement trod ;
>   As fresh as when the first sunrise
>   Awoke the lark in Paradise."

Let us live there, and it will not be hard to find illustrations !

XV

THE DEVOTIONAL SERVICE

IT seems fitting to say a few words under this heading, because the preacher has not only to deliver a sermon, but to conduct the preparatory worship, and the latter is perhaps of greater importance than the former. It is a loftier service to the people gathered in your congregation to conduct them into the presence of God, than even to deliver the message of God to their souls. It perhaps requires more spirituality, more anointing of the Holy Spirit, more preparation of heart, to induce the devotional frame, than it does to interest people in your theme or produce a definite impression for good on their hearts and lives.

1. There are some who lay great stress upon the unity of a service. If the theme of their sermon is a joyous one, they feel that they are bound to select passages of Scripture and hymns of a joyous, hopeful character. If, on the other hand, they desire in their sermon to comfort the sorrowful and distressed, the idea of comfort pervades all the

7

previous service. I was once as great an admirer of this manner of proceeding as anyone whom I may be addressing, but of late years I have seriously changed my mind, and it seems to me a mistake to allow the entire service, from beginning to end, to repeat one refrain.

It may be that into your congregation, when your heart is full of joy, there has strayed some weary soul needing the tender tones of consolation, or some perplexed child of God not knowing which way to take; or someone misunderstood and persecuted who needs direction. Is it not desirable to meet the case of such, which would not be touched by your subsequent exhortations, by affording in the hymn, prayer, or Scripture some appropriate help? The very fact that your keynote is joy, for instance, ought to make you think of those whose hearts are stricken and sorrowful, and you should provide for them in either hymn or Scripture. I am sure that every service ought to touch, as much as possible, the entire range of human need, and all the experience which may be represented by the faces before you.

By all means let the last hymn be carefully selected to bear out the impression of your sermon. You should always select this for yourself. As for the rest, I often leave the choice of hymns to others, that my people may be saved from perpetually singing those of my choosing, and may be led into other paths of our hymnology not so often trodden by my own feet. I quite admit that the dominant note of a service may be clearly accentuated, and may reappear again and again throughout its course, but I do urge that you will probably gather more force in the enunciation of your one lesson if there is variation, change, and modulation throughout your devotional service.

2. It is very desirable to be fairly deliberate in the introductory service. I do not mean that the prayers should be prolix, the Scripture lessons too long, or that anything should savour of tedium or weariness, but I have sometimes felt that there was an undue rush and haste. No sooner was the prayer over than the minister was giving out the hymn, and the people were hardly sitting down from singing before he had announced the Scripture. It seems to me that the soul needs time to turn from one act of devotion to another. A slight pause now and again, a deliberation in the approach to God, an interval during which the worshipper may take off the shoes from his feet because he stands on holy ground, give a sense of calm and peace which are an agreeable contrast to the rush and speed of ordinary life.

3. The liturgy of the Church of England gives the true method of public worship. It begins with

confession and the aspiration to stand before God accepted in the Beloved. Then it bursts into praise with its psalms and ancient hymns, and finally passes into litanies of intercession and supplication. These notes should never be wanting in our worship. We must always begin as those whose feet need washing, whose consciences need purification, whose robes must be fresh cleansed in the precious blood, and purged from all sin. The heart must be assured of pardon before it can plead with God for itself and others. There must be a conscious application on the part of the minister and people for the blood of cleansing. There must be bursts of praise and adoring love; there must be ladders up which the soul can climb to join with angels and archangels and all the company of heaven in praising and blessing God; and there must be opportunities for intercession and prayer on behalf of all sorts and conditions of men.

4. In reading the Scripture you must be very careful to study it beforehand, that you may know where to lay the emphasis, and how best to bring out the meaning by the inflections of your voice. How many texts in the Bible are almost nonsense read as they are ordinarily read! What a means of grace it is to hear an intelligent student of the Scriptures read well known and familiar passages; at every step new beauties flash into light.

You can stop and comment upon what you read if you will, but it needs consummate wisdom to do this well, else the Bible becomes diluted and watered down by human additions. For the most part, I think it is better to let God speak for Himself. Let there be an opportunity in your service for God the Lord to utter His voice through your lips; and be sure to read reverently, clearly, emphatically, and devoutly, that the people may understand the proclamation of the Great King.

It would well repay some of us to take lessons in elocution. I have taken more than one course, and wish that I had profited more by my opportunities. I remember, for instance, one of my masters telling me how necessary it was to use more of the rising inflection as I came to the termination of my sentences, because the falling inflection was apt to depress a congregation—a remark which I have never forgotten, and which has been of great service in the reading of God's Word. There are few things more uncommon than to hear the Bible well and properly read. It is the most difficult book in the world to read, because the verses break up the paragraphs, and the clauses, especially in St. Paul's writings, are linked together in such a close ascending series that only the very best elocutionists are able to carry the mind of the hearer from the beginning of the sentence, in un-

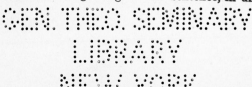

broken sequence, to the end. We ought to pray that God would help us to make the reading of the Scriptures a means of grace to our hearers. It would be well for some of us, on Saturday afternoons, to go into the place of worship where we are to preach on Sunday, and read the lessons from the desk, with some kind and wise listener who could criticise our style. By all means seek that the reading of the Bible should magnify the book in the estimation of your hearers.

The matter of public prayer is so important that I must reserve it for a separate paper. Probably there is no part of the service that needs more of the anointing of the Holy Spirit, more of the unction of the Holy One, more devout preparation of the heart. We do not pray instead of our people, like the Thibetan praying-mills, but we need to pray in such a way as to stir the slumbering embers of their devotion to break into a flame.

Looked at under these lights, ours is a high office. We are not priests, we do not stand between God and man, but we may take our brother man by the hand, and lead him into courts not made with hands, through worshipping throngs of holy beings, and stand side by side with them, uttering in unison words that move the heart of God.

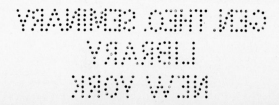

XVI

PUBLIC PRAYER

THERE is no part of the public service, especially among our Free Churches, more important, and demanding more careful thought and preparation beforehand, than the holy service we are called upon to render to the congregation in the expression of their prayers and desires before God. It is really easier to preach than to pray aright, easier to speak to man than take up the sorrow, care, and sin of a great congregation, in speaking with them to God. But what minister is there who will not confess that what the prayer is, the sermon is apt to be—that the prayer gives the keynote to the whole service? If it be inspiring, heaven-born, and heaven-ascending, it will lift the entire audience into the very presence of the King; whilst, if in prayer, we are desultory, wandering, and lacking in fervour, the whole service is likely to be impaired.

It is customary at this point for those who discuss the subject of public prayer to determine on the respective merits of a liturgy and of free

prayer. For myself, during the last ten years of
my life, I have felt it very helpful and refreshing
to join in the prayer of the magnificent liturgy of
the English Church, with certain alterations and
omissions. It has been a great comfort to me to
know that the needs of the people were being so
fitly and fully expressed, that there was nothing to
be desired; whilst the free prayer before the
sermon enabled me to add anything of a specific
or personal nature which the circumstances of the
congregation or the nation might seem to demand.
But this question hardly demands our attention
here, for the immense majority of those to whom
I am speaking, by the very nature of the case,
have no option than to lead their congregations
into the presence of God, their own words consti-
tuting the stairway of approach.

Let there be dignity in your public prayer. Do
not speak to God as though He were your next-
door neighbour. There may be the familiarity of a
child, but you must remember that your Father is
a great King. There is an abundance of becoming
phrases in the Psalms and the prophets, which
provide noble and spirit-moving conceptions of the
greatness of God, whilst the enumeration of His
attributes, the glory of His nature, the wonder of
His handiwork in creation, and the wisdom of His
providence are all so many arguments on which

we may rest the superstructure of supplication. It is a happy art to combine the freedom of a child in speaking to the Father with the reverence and decorum which become His presence whose greatness is unsearchable. One very much shrinks from the constant repetition of the name of Jesus apart from the befitting title of Lord; and anything approaching endearing terms, which we may use to our Saviour in the moments of private devotion, is to be carefully guarded. Only now and again, when our hearts have reached high-water mark, may we venture to address Him in such words as St. Bernard or Rutherford might have used.

Be comprehensive in your petitions. The aged and little children, the sick and the dying, the tempted and the lonely, sailors that go down to the sea in ships, and soldiers who may be fighting on the battlefield, public servants—as postmen and policemen—Christian workers of all grades should from time to time be remembered. It is not well, perhaps, to enumerate all of these in one prayer, lest it become prolix, and the mind of the worshippers be so weighted with the diversity of petition as to be unable to fix itself on any; but in the course of a month all these and many more conditions of human need should pass, in well-considered words, before the thought of the people.

It is well sometimes to run over the Litany of the
Church, to note if any cases are mentioned there
which are habitually absent from your own petitions;
and to this venerable and beautiful enumeration of
the circumstances of human need it is well from
time to time to add the suggestions of other litanies
and prayers, so that there may be a constant
novelty and freshness in the subjects which you
lay before God.   You hardly realise how glad
parents and relatives are to hear some specific
petition which recalls the absent son and brother.
The chalice of your prayer is at once filled with
the wine of their love.   Be sure to mention little
children, who will in this way have their attention
kept awake until their presence is acknowledged,
and the parents will gladly recognise that the
whole congregation is helping them to bear the
burden which is never very far away from their
thought.

It is good to keep a sheet of paper on the
mantelpiece of your room, where during the week
you may jot down any special subject for prayer
which may be suggested by the newspaper or the
current life around.   To glance down this list
before entering the pulpit is eminently suggestive.
At the same time it is necessary to avoid making
the public prayer a kind of notice board, from
which all the gossips of the congregation may

obtain items for discussion. You must take care
to guard against starting people's minds on a series
of questions as to what family or individual may
have been referred to. This will bring down the
temperature of the entire church, for everyone
becomes aware when those around have ceased to
pray.

Be wise in ordering the length of prayer. I was
taking the morning service at one of the largest of
our churches in England on a recent Sunday, and
was asked in the vestry by the assistant minister if
I would umdertake the *long prayer.* I said I would
be very happy, *only I was afraid I could not pray
long enough.* I have been told that the prayers in
some of our churches will extend to fifteen or
twenty minutes. Against such undue prolixity I
enter my protest. There are very few minds that
can sustain such an intense act for so long, for in
prayer the understanding, the emotions, the sense
of the Unseen and Eternal, to the exclusion of the
transient, must be kept at high pressure, and it is
simply impossible to expect so much of a great
congregation, containing many of infirm minds,
many who are weary and tired with the work of
the week, many boys and girls, who become more
and more restless.

In my judgment a brief dedicatory prayer at the
beginning of the service, a prayer of confession and

personal supplication, and a third prayer of intercession, are infinitely preferable to one long prayer, and I urge this division upon my brethren. I am met by the reply of some that they cannot arouse themselves to intense supplication unless they have time for the brain to acquire momentum; but I think this applies probably more to private than to public prayer, and that it is more profitable on the whole to have the variety which I have suggested as a stimulus to the minds and hearts of the congregation.

We must guard against anything which diverts the thoughts of our people from God to ourselves, our language, or our thought. We have all heard the story of the man who offered the finest prayer ever presented to a Boston audience, and we have often been tempted to remember the story when we have heard some magniloquent address to the Almighty, accompanied by discussions on doctrine and expositions of truth which were as far from the true conception of prayer as the east is from the west. We have no right to call attention in public prayer to our diction, our views of doctrine, our cleverness or ingenuity. We have no right to air our views on political matters, or to take some mean revenge upon those with whom we differ. Our words should be as transparent as the ether itself. Just as on the Mediterranean coast or in Syria the

light is so intense that all colour seems to stand
out in unrivalled picturesqueness and distinctness,
so our words, without attracting attention to themselves, should set forth simply and clearly our
desires towards God, dealing with Him as so very
near that the congregation finds itself transported
into His presence, and the heavenly horizons are as
clearly defined as those by which individual lives
are daily limited.

There ought to be some order in public prayer.
Praise should mingle with supplication, confession of
sins with yearnings after holiness. Supplications
for the individual, the home, the Church, and the
nation should not be wanting. Prayer for mis-
sionaries and native converts should always have a
place. Sometimes one order may be adopted, and
at other times another, but on the whole there
must always be first the confession of sin, and then
the outburst of thanksgiving and intercession.

Does the task of public prayer appal you? Do
you feel as though the ideal suggested is too high
for you to attain? Are you tempted to exclaim,
" Who is sufficient for these things? " Then remember that the Spirit helpeth your infirmities,
and that the great High Priest waits to mingle
His intercession with yours, and to present them
ordered and perfected in the presence of the Father.
We can never forget the vision given of Him by

the apostle, who tells us that He stands before the altar having a golden censer, and that there is given unto Him much incense, that He may add it unto the prayers of all the saints upon the golden altar which is before the throne (Rev. viii. 3, 4).

Do not let people speak to you of many things before you enter the pulpit. Let there be a look on your face which shall compel silence and reverence in the vestry, because there is a great awe on your heart. You are going to speak to God for men, and to men for God. Have, if possible, a little audible prayer before going forth on this great errand.

XVII

FAULTS TO GUARD AGAINST

EVERY calling in life has its own peculiar pitfalls and snares, and those which beset the life of the minister are very insidious and persistent. Never until the end of life are we free from our liability to any one of the weaknesses and failings which are mentioned in the following paragraphs. We may never put off our armour, never throw ourselves on the sward to rest, never allow ourselves to suppose that the enemy has finally retired from the field. The test which Gideon employed was a perfectly just one, when he insisted that the men who cast themselves upon the bank to drink, though the foe might be anywhere within a mile or two, were not the men who should deliver Israel. Those who stood alert upon the river bank, catching up the water in the hollow of their hand, ready to meet the foe at any moment, proved themselves to be men of the true temper for his great purpose.

The first failing to guard against is an undue and wanton familiarity with holy things. Our

hearers sometimes look up at us and think that, as
we are perpetually having intercourse with sacred
subjects, we must necessarily be ourselves as imbued
and saturated with the divine truth as the materials
that lie asoak in the mixture of the dyer's vat.
They say to themselves: "We, too, could be good,
if we were perpetually in contact with God and
heaven, if the Bible were perpetually in our hands,
and the materials of holy thought lay all around."
Ah! they do not know the fatal snare upon the
other side. It is just because we are always dealing with the vessels of the sanctuary that we are apt
to lose that fine sense of reverence which we felt
when first we entered the pulpit, first addressed an
audience in the name of God, and first pointed
an inquirer, impressed with our words, to the
Redeemer.

To some of us the opportunity comes of preaching at least once or twice on Sunday, and in some
cases of standing up for God ten or twelve times in
a week. It is inevitable that we should be tempted
to presume upon our familiarity with pulpit themes.
The spirit of mere professionalism peeps over our
shoulder, and an air of self-confident assurance
settles down on our face and bearing. We find
no difficulty in offering public prayer, for we have
only to repeat the well-worn sentences which have
so often passed our lips. We do not tremble as

we stand up with the awful message of the grace or terror of God, because we are so sure that as we have never broken down we shall never break down ; because we have always secured a moderate meed of success, therefore we may count pretty certainly upon passing muster with the majority of the people. Too often there is a kind of jauntiness which is very offensive. While we are in the pulpit we may appear dignified and solemn, but there was a lightness in manner and speech before we entered it which will be resumed when we again reach the vestry. Our habitual use and wont have blunted the edge of the razor and taken off the fine bloom from the fruit.

I do not know how this can be guarded against, except by receiving each sermon as a definite message from God, and engaging in devout and earnest intercession before we deliver it. A few words of prayer uttered in the vestry before we leave it are better than nothing, but they ought not to take the place of very definite waiting upon God, of very deep and profound entreaty that the soul may be anointed with fresh oil, and of very intense sympathy with the awful state of souls that may be in that congregation—slipping back into sin, standing on the brink of temptation, or absolutely dead in trespasses and sins. There must be fresh ammunition and fresh power for every service.

8

The second of these failings is the absence of passion in our soul. I was struck with the leading article in a daily paper which I came across the other day. The burden of it was as follows :—

The greatest oratory is not only without decorations, but it is that kind of speaking which, without being of the highest merit, is at anyrate downright in earnest. Ornamental oratory is poor oratory, and for the purpose of persuading and inspiring, it is weak and ineffective. The true note of powerful speaking is passion, and passion rushes along the shortest and simplest line to its goal. In the speeches which Milton puts into the mouths of the speakers in the debate in Pandemonium there is not a single formal metaphor. The diction is that of severe prose, and the verses are as compact as diamonds, and as bright ; not a word is wasted, the meaning is clear, and the arguments tell for all they are worth. Demosthenes' oration on the Crown contains scarcely a single ornamental jewel. So in Shakespeare, who looked at life through the golden haze of romance—the more earnest the speakers become, the plainer and simpler their orations, as, for instance, those of Brutus and Anthony after the murder of Cæsar. They are winged words, but the pinions do not come from metaphor, but from intense passion. And so it always, or nearly always, is : where deep passion exists, where there is an intense, or even a strong conviction, a sense of the gravity of the crisis, a burning desire to arouse, to persuade, to sway, to guide, the speaking will throb with power, its argument will come like cannon balls, and its passion will scathe like lightning.

Perhaps few men can rise to this height, and yet for want of it our preaching becomes colourless and uninfluential. A man may not speak with grammatical accuracy, or a wide choice of words, but if he speak with the passion of intense feeling he is a great speaker, and men will be compelled to listen to him. The fire that burns in his heart will be contagious, and will make all hearts glow. Whilst, on the other hand, a man may use perfectly turned and exquisitely balanced sentences, gems may sparkle in every paragraph, the argument may be effectively presented, but if, with all this, there is no passion, no intensity, no fire, the people go away unmoved, the conscience is not gripped, the heart is hardly touched.

It was this power of passion which must have given to Dr. Chalmers the marvellous gift which he exercised in his ministry, when the Glasgow merchants waited in the reading-rooms not far from the Tron Church, that they might rush out at the first tinkle of the kirk bell, and secure a place for the great weekly sermon, at the height of the

working day; when the students claimed remission
of the fine for non-attendance at their classes on the
ground that they had gone to hear Dr. Chalmers;
when the busy people of every condition snatched
an hour at noon from their labours to hear the
great voice in their midst; when every man's
breathing was suspended as the mighty sentences
rolled forth, not in the necessary service of Sunday,
but in the middle of the week, in an hour which
was worth money to the energetic and money-
making community. Then for an hour every breath
was held, every cough suppressed, while each hearer
restrained himself under the spell of the impassioned
and entrancing eloquence; and a great sigh burst
from the overcharged bosoms of the multitude when
the oration came to an end. What a record that is
that he makes in a jotting of his diary: "Preached
in the Gorbals in the afternoon, *and exceeded* in the
pulpit."

It is not to be inferred that I am advocating
here anything of mere declamation, or excitement,
or vehement gesture, but intensity,—that the whole
nature may be gathered up into one supreme act in
the deliverance of the divine message, upon which
the eternal destiny of souls may be depending.
May God Himself infuse into our hearts a
passion for His glory, a passion for the souls of
men, a passion for the coming of the Redeemer's

kingdom, that our words may glow and burn like coals.

The third failure or weakness against which we must be on our guard is the habit of superficiality. We are all tempted to be lazy. It is possible to spend two or three hours in the study, surrounded by books, flitting like a butterfly from one to another, but girding ourselves to no great effort of thought. It is here that the pen comes in to test us. We have often found that it is possible to read listlessly one book after another, absorbing the thoughts of others, without bringing one's mind into distinct and living contact with the truths which they may be discussing. It is so easy to allow oneself to feed on milk, which is food that has passed through the digestion of another, without exerting oneself to wrestle with the angel of truth in the dark until we extort his secret.

It is always better to give a little truth which we have personally discovered and hammered out in our own workshop, like the beaten work of the cherubim of old, than to give much of the results of other men's researches. Use the pen, write as you think. Even if there is no prospect of using what you write in the written form in public, yet the very habit of writing will compel you to think, and crystallise the results of your reading.

It is in this way that we discover whether we

are merely glancing over the surface of things or
dealing with their heart. All public speakers are
tempted to be superficial, to talk to their people
generally, to sketch out great continents of truth
without staying to fill in countries, mountains, or
rivers; to suggest rather than to inform; to give
an appearance of wide information without the less
attractive work of subsoil ploughing. It is not
so difficult to talk for an hour about some Bible
character if we have had the opportunity of scanning
slightly two or three articles from various biblical
encyclopædias and commentaries; but there may be
no vigorous thinking, no grappling with the problems of life, no effort of our own to portray the
figure on the canvas in the aspect in which he
presents himself to the peculiar standpoint of our
thought.

*The fourth weakness against which we must
guard is the tendency always to make use of old
materials.* Of course there is no reason why we
should not preach an old sermon if we preach with
a fresh anointing, a fresh perception of God, a fresh
contact with the truth it presents. But it is a
solemn thing for a man to be always preaching his
old sermons. Nothing will more certainly indicate
his degeneracy. That a growing child should be
able to wear, year after year, the same clothes, is
a sign that his health is seriously declining. In

mature life, of course, we wear clothes made from the same tailor's measurements; there is no need to alter from year to year; but in the moral and spiritual realm we never reach our maturity—we are always children growing from less to more. To be always preaching the same sermons is to indicate that we have ceased to develop, and to cease to grow is practically to die.

The temptation to preach an old sermon is not so imminent to those of us who have settled pulpits, for our people are quick enough to remember any sermon which has already arrested them (even though we should choose another text!) But the temptation presses upon those who are perpetually moving about, and who have only to turn their bundle of sermons upside down, and start again to preach through the entire pack. It may thus befall that one or two hundred discourses or less will, by repeated use, be made to spread over the preaching opportunities of an entire life. It is important that we should produce one new sermon for every five occasions of an intinerant ministry, in order to keep our perceptive and inventive faculties from perishing through disuse. It is good to wait before God in the morning of any day in which we are to be called to minister to the people, to ask of Him what message He wishes to be delivered, and then deliver it fresh and hot, like the show-bread which every week was laid upon the golden table of the sanctuary.

The last weakness and temptation against which we must guard is that of a fancied superiority over others. The temptation of the pulpit is to make a man autocratic, and impatient of the criticism and discussion through which the words of every man must necessarily pass before they can be received as the current coin of the world. In the pulpit, there is no one to dispute what we say. When the sermon is over, those who disagree with us vent their grumblings on their wives and friends, out of our hearing, whilst only those who adore us are admitted to the inner shrine, to stand around with their flattering speech. We judge ourselves by what those who love us say; we look at ourselves through their eyes. Those who take an independent position, and offer the slightest criticism, are not welcomed into the sacred circle of our court. Those who differ from us are made to feel the wintry side of the street. We wrap ourselves up in our most warmly lined coats when the cold blast of adverse criticism approaches us. All this generates a habit of proud self-opinionativeness which is extremely harmful. It would be good for us, if, like some of our English kings, we could disguise ourselves as ordinary people and mix in the affairs of men. It would be good if we joined debating societies, where our opinions would be ruthlessly convassed and our oracular speeches mercilessly torn to shreds. We might have to hear things which would be hard of digestion, but most salutary, and through the knowing of which we might rise up into a truer appreciation of the divine word on the one hand, and of human need on the other.

Do let us guard against being little popes, against an autocratic insistence on our ways of thinking or stating the truth, and against an oracular announcement of our opinion on all matters in heaven and on earth. Humility, teachableness, converse with our fellows, the reading of the daily press, and, above all, fellowship with God, are the superlative correctives for any tendency to think of ourselves more highly than we ought to think. Let us remember the Master's words, "He that would be first, let him be least of all, and servant of all."

> " There is a secret place of rest
>   God's saints alone may know ;
> Thou shalt not find it east nor west,
>   Though seeking to and fro.
> A cell where Jesus is the door,
>   His love the only key ;
> Who enter will go out no more,
>   But there with Jesus be."

XVIII

YOUR CHARGE OF YOURSELF

WE are often told of a minister's charge of his congregation, but the greatest charge of all is his own character. This arises from the fact that what we are so largely affects what we say. If our people have any suspicion that there is a rift, however slight, between our teaching and our daily living, between our religious phraseology and our practical morality, we may speak with the tongues of angels, but they refuse to be captivated. It is not so much what we say, but what we are, that weighs with our people. They will be only too apt to discount our sermons if they are conscious that there is any laxity in our personal or domestic habit. "Take heed to thyself, and to thy doctrine," said the apostle, "for thus thou shalt save thyself and them that hear thee."

The character of the minister largely affects that of his people. It is not without profound significance that the letters to the seven churches are inscribed to their respective *angels*, a title which probably designates their chief teacher and spiritual guide. In addressing the minister, the great Head of the Church knew that He was touching on the salient features of the life of the people committed to his care. It is impossible that people should concentrate their attention on their minister for so many hours each week without insensibly taking an impression of his character as well as of his instructions.

In addition to all this, we must remember that God does not undertake to use instruments which have become contaminated by wilfully committed sin. He will not put His throne-water into polluted vessels. He may hide His heavenly treasures in earthen vessels, but not in unclean ones. He is prepared to walk in fellowship with those who are far from perfect, so long as they are perpetually applying for cleansing in the blood of Christ, but He refuses to work with those whose hands and hearts are persistently soiled by abominable things which He hates. Surely the fact that He calls us to work with Him should induce in ourselves a reverent habit of life, that we should always work out, with fear and trembling, that which He works in, and that we should regard with profound reverence the nature which He designs to make a vehicle for His communications with His children.

There is a profoundly interesting narrative in the Book of Leviticus which illustrates the necessity of personal holiness. It was only a week since Aaron and his four sons had been consecrated to the priestly office. Sin offerings and burnt offerings had inaugurated their entrance on their sacred work. The blood and oil had touched various parts of their bodies, in token of their consecration to the service of the sanctuary, and specific injunctions had been laid upon them. The father and sons had just entered upon their official functions when an awful catastrophe took place, and Nadab and Abihu were stretched out in death, suddenly smitten by the hand of God. And what was the reason? It may be, as the ninth verse suggests, that they had taken stimulants to nerve them for the august duties to which they were summoned; or, it may be that they were wilfully and presumptuously negligent of the precision of the divine commandment. But, in any case, they had offered strange fire upon the altar in defiance of the divinely prescribed method. "Then Moses said unto Aaron, This is it that the Lord spake, saying, I will be sanctified in them that come nigh Me, and before all the people I will be glorified."

Instead of taking the fire needed for their censers from the brazen altar, they seem to have made use of common fire, and thus committed an act which, considering the descent of the miraculous fire they had so recently witnessed, and the solemn obligation laid upon them to make use of the heaven-sent flame in the service of the altar, betrayed a carelessness, irreverence, and want of faith which could not but have a prejudicial effect upon the whole nation, needing to be taught the first elementary law of literal obedience.

How often have we been guilty of the same sin ? There is but one fire—that of the baptism of the Holy Spirit—that should burn upon the altar of our heart, and spread from us to others. The absence of that sacred fire cannot be concealed, and its presence may not be simulated. Yet how often we have made use of the strange fire of human excitement, of fervid manner, of vehement gesticulation, of mere emotional address ! Sometimes, when we have been most conscious that the Spirit of God has been wanting in our ministrations, we have tried to atone for the lack of His gracious influence by some abnormal manifestation of merely human activities. Strange fire has been kindled in our censers, and strange fire has been communicated to our people.

We cannot be too careful of ourselves, for it is only as we are separated from known sin, that God will call us into the mountain to speak with us face to face. This charge of our own souls, this care of our own vineyard, this tillage of our own field, demands, and must have, soul leisure, quietness, calm, and concentration of spirit. Earth's voices must be silenced that we may be able to hear God's still, small voice, warning, convincing, condemning, admonishing. He is waiting for those who have leisure to draw near to Him, and it is becoming on our part to give Him the opportunity of opening His secret thoughts and counsels with respect to us, lest we become like the foolish prophets described by Ezekiel, " who follow their own spirit, and have seen nothing" (Ezek. xiii. 2–17).

There are three traits of which we must be specially careful.

(1) *Humility.* Beware of a pseudo-humility which is of the lips rather than of the heart, which bemoans, in loud tones, its wretchedness and helplessness, and takes the opportunity of attracting notice by its very expressions of lowliness and unworthiness. You will not find these things in a truly humble person. As another has said, " A man or woman upon whom God has bestowed the true grace of humility sometimes appears to have an amount of self-reliance and confidence, the source of which is not evident, but which is simply the result of entire and absolute dependence upon God." Such a person is as ready to do the smallest thing, unknown and unnoticed

of men, as to undertake some difficult, and, to the
world, apparently ambitious enterprise, for the
cause of the Master and for the service of man.
He is not at all apt to talk about his own weakness, or to proclaim and bewail his own unfitness.
He is too humble to think about these things; he
lives absolutely in the dust in the presence of Him
whose instrument he is, and who chooses things
which are not to bring to nought things that are.
Let us cultivate this spirit that lies low before God,
accountable to Him alone, conscious of being able
to do, and effect, nothing of ourselves, but asking
Him to work in us and through us. Let us seek
the honour that cometh from God only, that our
mind and heart be occupied exclusively with
Him.

(2) *Purity.* There is no grace which so absolutely captivates and holds the admiration of men
as habitual self-restraint, that the whole being shall
be kept in hand, not because it is wanting in
the element human feeling, but because every
thought and emotion is brought into captivity to
Jesus Christ. It must never be forgotten that
often those who are most susceptible towards God
are most easily overcome by the sins of the flesh.
In proportion, therefore, as we are conscious of
being able to mount into the heights of holy
fellowship and service, we must beware of the

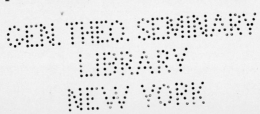

other possibility, of being hurled into the darkest abyss of pollution.

(3) *Prayerfulness.* Here is the weapon by which we are able to conquer in the lonely inner fight, through which each of us must pass. Joshua went forth alone to meditate by Jericho, and there encountered the Captain of the Lord's host. We, too, must go forth to stand by ourselves in the midst of the conflict which is ever raging between light and darkness, Christ and Antichrist.

It is then we shall be conscious that Emanuel, our Captain, is leading the hosts of God. We shall also be conscious of the hostility of the principalities and powers of darkness. Then it is we must pray. In prayer we take sides; in prayer we cast the whole weight of ourselves for good against evil, for purity against impurity, for Christ against the devil. We must learn to pour out our souls before God. We must see to it that the Spirit of God is able to intercede within us with groanings that cannot be uttered, not for our flock only, but that in our lonely watch we may be preserved from the lion and the bear, and enabled so to live that we may meet the Chief Shepherd at His coming without shame.